"You're Back," Deke Murmured,

and turned her into his arms.

There was a raw hunger in his kiss that seemed to eat at her very soul. Angie strained close, pressing herself to his entire length, her arms wound tightly around his neck. The crush of his arms was an exquisite pain she could have endured for an endless time, but he drew away. Angie lowered her gaze, not willing for him to see the love she guessed was in her eyes.

"How long before I can see her, Deke?" If he loved her, he wouldn't keep her separated from her daughter. She had to test him.

Anger flashed in his gray eyes. "Don't push it, Angie," he warned.

JANET DAILEY
having lived in so many locales, has come to know the people of America. She has written 65 books selling more than 80 million copies, and she'll be writing many more for Silhouette in the future. Her husband, Bill, is actively involved in doing all the research for Janet's books. They make their home in Branson, Missouri.

Dear Reader,

Silhouette Special Editions are an exciting new line of contemporary romances from Silhouette Books. Special Editions are written specifically for our readers who want a story with heightened romantic tension.

Special Editions have all the elements you've enjoyed in Silhouette Romances and *more*. These stories concentrate on romance in a longer, more realistic and sophisticated way, and they feature greater sensual detail.

I hope you enjoy this book and all the wonderful romances from Silhouette. We welcome any suggestions or comments and invite you to write to us at the address below.

Editor-in-Chief,
Silhouette Books,
P.O. Box 910,
517 Lorne Ave.,
Stratford, Ontario N5A 6W3

JANET DAILEY
Terms of Surrender

Silhouette Special Edition

Published by Silhouette Books New York

Distributed in Canada by PaperJacks Ltd., a Licensee
of the trademarks of Simon & Schuster, a division of
Gulf+Western Corporation.

Other Silhouette Books by Janet Dailey

The Hostage Bride
The Lancaster Men
For The Love of God
Wildcatter's Woman
Foxfire Light

SILHOUETTE BOOKS, a Simon & Schuster Division of
GULF & WESTERN CORPORATION
1230 Avenue of the Americas, New York, N.Y. 10020
In Canada distributed by PaperJacks Ltd.,
330 Steelcase Road, Markham, Ontario.

ISBN: 0-671-53501-3

First Silhouette Books printing February, 1982

10 9 8 7 6 5 4

Printed in Canada

Terms of
Surrender

Chapter One

$\mathcal{T}$ he state highway started its scenic curve around the Ski Basin, its waters calm and reflecting the blue of a Texas sky. Angie Hall slowed her blue Pinto car, an action not dictated by the approach to the Rockport business district or any speed limits. As she rolled down the window on the driver's side, she caught the tangy scent of Gulf air. A gull's cry sounded apart from the noise of the highway traffic.

Her hands gripped the car's steering wheel until her knuckles showed white. At the split in the road, Angie took the business route rather than the bypass around the downtown district. She parked her car in the first available space along the main street and remained behind the wheel for a long moment just staring at the sights that had changed so little in seven years.

Someone strolled along the sidewalk and sent a curious glance inside the car, prodding Angie into an awareness of how long she had sat, unmoving. Extracting the key from the ignition, she glanced out the window for oncoming traffic, then climbed out of her car, not bothering to lock it.

Nothing was coming so she quickly jaywalked across the street. The click-click of her backless heels on the pavement echoed behind her and made it seem as if someone was following her, but it was only the past and its memories. Angie paused on the other side, then moved slowly toward the small harbor. White designer jeans showed off the length of her legs and the eye-catching curve of her hips. The short-sleeved velour top of garnet red was less revealing of her figure, only hinting at the fullness of her breasts.

The salty breath of a Gulf breeze moved familiarly over her as if in rediscovery. There was almost a caressing quality to it as it tangled itself in the amber length of her hair and whispered over her face. Inwardly, Angie struggled against the sensation while her smooth features remained unusually expressionless, determined not to reveal the brittle tension within, but there was a troubled darkness in her indigo eyes, an uncertainty and apprehension.

As she neared the small harbor, the freshness of the salt air became tainted with a pungent fishy smell. Most of it was caused by the short row of bait shops, but some of it drifted from the shrimp boats at the docks. Angie wandered closer to them, drawn by an invisible force. A brown pelican was perched on the bow of one of the shrimp boats, but Angie didn't notice it or the screeching gulls overhead.

The long arms that held the shrimp nets at sea, were upraised, a certain starkness to their line. But her mind flashed back to that summer seven years ago when boats such as these were gaily festooned with decorations for the annual Blessing of the Shrimp Fleet. It was part of the "Shrimporee" celebration in the larger community of Aransas Pass, just down the road from Rockport. Those July days had been such fun-filled times that summer, dominated by a reckless, devil-may-care attitude. When a girl is seventeen, it's so easy to forget there's a tomorrow.

Angie turned sharply away from the shrimp boats, wanting to shut out from her mind what had come after the celebrations. She had spent seven years shutting it out—so what was she doing here? But Angie refused to acknowledge the question. Instinct was a primal thing that dictated its own course of action.

It was a gesture of inner tension that lifted her hand to push the blond hair off her cheek as Angie circled to the front of the bait shops that also booked charter fishing excursions. She absently read their signboards, absorbing none of the words. The late morning sun was warm in the subtropical climate of the Texas Gulf Coast, even though it was November.

"Could I interest you in a charter, miss?" A man's voice drawled to her left. "We've had some real good luck lately deep-sea fishing."

A middle-aged man with a thickening waistline leaned an elbow on the jutting edge of an exterior counter a few paces ahead of Angie. A dingy white captain's hat was perched atop his silvering dark hair and his navy blue windbreaker was unzipped. His benign features had a weathered look from years of sun and sea. The inquiry was more of a friendly overture to start a conversation than an outright attempt to hawk his ware.

Angie responded, accepting the distraction conversation offered. "Not this time, I'm afraid." She half-smiled and idled in front of the bait stand. "It certainly is a beautiful day for it, though," she said with a glance at the clear sky overhead.

"Couldn't be better," he agreed, then eyed her with a mildly inquisitive look. "Do you live around here or are you on holiday?"

A wariness claimed her even though Angie knew the man was attempting to pry. "On holiday," she admitted and quickly added, "just passing through on my way to Corpus Christi and on down to the valley." She was unnecessarily forceful about the clarification of her plans, stating them firmly to remind herself.

"You might want to take a look around this

area before driving all that way. It has a lot to offer," he insisted in praise of his own community. "And it's not so crowded. 'Course, in a couple weeks, the 'snowbirds' will be flocking in all up and down the coast." After a slight pause, he explained, "'Snowbirds' is the name we give to all the folks who come south to spend the winter."

Her smile was stiff. "I've heard the term before." She didn't give him a chance to ask how she knew it and hurried to elaborate on her vacation plans. "Once I reach Brownsville, I thought I'd cross the border into Mexico and do some shopping. I've been told a person can find a lot of bargains there."

"And that's something no woman can resist." The man smiled broadly.

"I guess not," Angie admitted, not caring that she was perpetuating a myth about her sex. She suddenly had no desire to continue the conversation, not even sure why she had begun it in the first place. She took an initial step to move away. "I'd better be on my way."

"You have a safe trip." The friendly fishing boat captain made no attempt to detain her, lifting a hand in a half-salute.

"Thanks." Her reply was almost absent as Angie turned away and began retracing her steps to the parked car.

While she waited at the curb for the oncoming traffic to go by, she caught herself intently studying each vehicle in search of a familiar one. With a self-reproving shake of her head, she quit looking. That was crazy. No one would be driving the same car for seven years and least of all Deke Blackwood. Forget. Forget. Forget. The word drummed in her head, its cadence familiar from long repetition.

There was a gap in the flow of traffic and Angie darted across the street to her waiting car, sliding into the driver's seat and slamming the door. She glanced in the rear-view mirror and saw the reflection of an attractive, self-contained woman of twenty-four. Angie knew the secrets hidden behind those dark blue eyes, the events of the past that haunted her. The decision she'd made seven years ago had been the practical one—the logical one—the sensible one; given the same set of circumstances, she would probably make the same decision again—so why couldn't she accept it?

Driven by a self-impatience, Angie started the engine and made an abrupt U-turn in the middle of the street, leaving the business district behind and traveling the state highway once more. It was several minutes before she realized where she was going. By then, Angie had already made the turn that would take her out to the Key. She surrendered to the impulse to see the house where she had stayed with her aunt that summer seven years ago. Looking across the inlet, she could see the land had been greatly developed in the interim with townhouses and condominiums as well as private homes. The yacht basin was filled with boats of varying shapes and sizes.

Before reaching the bridge that would take her across to the Key, Angie passed a grove of live oak trees. The prevailing breeze from the Gulf had picturesquely sculpted the trees, bending them over and raking their limbs over their lowered tops. It was a common sight along the Texas Gulf Coast—more typical than the palm trees that dotted the residential lawns on the Key.

Even though it had been seven years since she'd been to her aunt's house and a multitude of new ones had sprung up around it, Angie had no difficulty in locating it. Raised on stilts to protect it from a storm's waves, the house was painted an egg-shell blue instead of the sea green her aunt had chosen. Tricycles and toys were scattered over its driveway and lawn, revealing the house's present owners had young children. Angie slowed the car to a stop at the curb to look.

Within seconds her gaze was drawn to the large Spanish-style dwelling on the corner lot across the street. A canal ran behind it, allowing homeowners to dock their boats virtually in their backyards. There was an empty look to the house, an unlived-in quality. Angie wasn't surprised since it was only a summer home for the Blackwoods, a place near the Gulf to escape the inland heat. During the rest of the year, it wasn't used.

Staring, she sat behind the wheel of the car, the engine idling. One of the neighbors noticed the strange car at the curb and came to investigate its occupant. Angie wasn't aware of the man's approach until he bent to peer in the driver's window.

"Are you trying to find a certain address, miss?" he inquired, polite yet wary.

"No. That is—" Realizing that her behavior might seem suspicious, she explained, "My aunt, Lillie Beth Franklin, used to live in this house several years ago. I was in the area so I thought I'd come by to see if the place had changed much."

Between her explanation and her respectable, as well as attractive appearance, the aging gentleman was no longer concerned about the reason for her presence. "I imagine you see a lot of change. Houses have sprung up like mushrooms out here."

"They certainly have," Angie agreed, and let her gaze wander back to the red-tiled roof of the house on the opposite corner. "Do the Blackwoods still own the hacienda-style home over there?"

"They do," he nodded. "'Course, they only open it in the summer. The rest of the year it's shut. They own a big ranch outside of town aways." The man gave her a considering look. "Were you a friend of the Blackwoods?"

Angie hesitated, a lot of things trembling on the edge of her tongue, but only one escaped. "Marissa Blackwood and I are about the same age. We used to pal around together when I visited my aunt."

"A lovely young woman." His head bobbed in approval. His brown golfer's cap reminded

14

Angie of a cork. "Warm and friendly. You should stop by the ranch and see her."

Angie flexed her fingers and curled them tightly around the steering wheel. "We've lost touch over the years," she said by way of an indirect reply to his suggestion. Overcome with a sudden restlessness, she flashed the man a quick smile. "I guess I'd better be going before I'm accused of loitering. It was nice talking to you."

"My pleasure. Strictly my pleasure."

The man straightened as Angie shifted the car into gear and pulled away from the curb. After crossing the bridge, she headed back to the highway. This time she passed the inter-section to the business district of Rockport. She'd traveled only a few blocks when she noticed an old-time service station that had been converted into a short-order café specia-lizing in Texas barbeque. It had been the site of one of her favorite hangouts that summer. There was an "Open" sign in the window.

With it almost noon time, Angie flipped on the car's turn signals and crossed the lane to park next to the building. Leaving the car, she entered the little café. It had changed so little that it was all poignantly familiar to her, although she didn't recognize the couple working behind the counter.

Two customers were ahead of her—work-men by their clothes. While she waited her turn, Angie looked around the small inte-rior. The table and four chairs by the window had been "their" table. She and Deke had sat on the side facing the door, and his sister Marissa and her boyfriend—what was his name? Kyle? Cobb? Angie couldn't remember. There was only a dim image of a boyish-looking face and dark hair.

"What can I get for you, ma'm?"

Half-startled, Angie turned to face the man on the opposite side of the counter. She had to check the impulse to say "the usual." "Sliced barbeque beef sandwich and a Coke."

She watched him slice a portion of meat from the succulent beef brisket. The outside had been seared to hold in the natural juices, then coated with a tangy sauce, and cooked slowly until it was fork-tender. Angie became aware of the appetizing aromas that filled the little café. There was nothing like a Texas barbeque. Deke had told her it was because the meat was cooked over mesquite wood, its smoke adding a unique flavor to the meat—so she recalled.

After paying for her order, Angie carried the tray with her sandwich and drink away from the counter. No one was seated at "their" table, but she walked to a smaller one. The food tasted as good as she remembered it had, yet after a couple of bites, her appetite fled. She didn't know whether to blame the empty table by the window or the sudden freshness of her memories. She forced down a couple more bites, then gave up, nearly bolting from the café.

Once in the car, she drove away somewhat blindly. Her palms were sweating and her stomach seemed to churn with tension. She paid little attention to where she was going. All her actions seemed to be automatic, not needing conscious direction.

It was something of a jolt when Angie discovered the car was motionless, and the motor switched off. She looked around, catching her breath and holding it when she saw the elementary school across the way. She suddenly realized that all her previous stops had been leading up to this moment. She had been gathering her nerve to come here.

She left the car and crossed the street to the school's entrance. It was lunch period and the schoolyard was crowded with young children. Their laughter and shouts tugged at her. She lingered to watch them at play, studying their carefree faces for a long moment before entering the building.

Her first stop was the principal's office. Angie was quaking with nervous tremors as the secretary/receptionist rose from her desk. The plump woman's expression was friendly, but inquisitive.

"Hello. I'm Angie . . . Smith. I used to live here when I was younger." Which was a half-truth—just as the name she'd given was. Angie forced a lightness into her voice, attempting to hide the intense strain that threatened to break her. "I've been revisiting some of my old haunts and wondered if it would be all right if I wandered around the building." When the woman hesitated, Angie added, "I won't be staying long—less than half an hour. And I promise not to disrupt or intrude on any classes."

After an inspecting glance, the woman smiled. "I see no harm in it."

"Thank you." Angie began retreating from the office, tension knotting her stomach.

The hallways seemed to contain a waiting silence. As she walked along the corridor, the noise made by the high heels of her sandal shoes was a definite intrusion. She was gripped by the sensation that she should leave before it was too late, that she should forget everything and walk away while she could. Every logical, practical, sensible bone in her body told her to do just that, but she was driven by an instinct much more elemental and primitive.

Her steps slowed when she reached the door to the first grade classroom. It stood open. Angie hesitated for several tense seconds before venturing inside. There was no one in the room, although it was evident the abandonment was only temporary. Angie wandered to the rows of desks, her fingers trailing across a smooth top. Preoccupied, she didn't hear the approach of footsteps outside the door.

"Hi?" There was a questioning inflection to the greeting by a female's voice. Angie pivoted sharply, alarm showing briefly, then disappearing when she saw the slender brunette in the doorway. "Were you looking for Miss Graves?"

"Miss Graves?" The name meant nothing to Angie, and for an instant, she couldn't understand why the young woman thought she would be looking for that person.

"Yes. Miss Graves teaches the first grade class." The explanation was accompanied by a curious study of Angie. "I thought since you were in her room that you must be looking for her."

"No, I . . ." Angie paused and began to move slowly toward the doorway where the woman stood. She was only a few years older than Angie. "I used to live here years ago." She fell back on the explanation she had given the secretary in the principal's office.

There was an instant smile of understanding. "Revisiting some of your childhood stomping grounds, huh?" the brunette guessed.

"Yes, you could say that," Angie agreed.

"I'm Mrs. Lucy Gonzales, in charge of the second graders." The young woman introduced herself.

"I'm Angie . . . Smith," she faltered, almost forgetting the false surname she'd previously given, even though no one here was likely to remember an Angie Hall.

"Are you visiting relatives?" The young teacher wasn't trying to probe, merely expressing a friendly interest.

Blond hair brushed her shoulders at the negative shake of her head. "No. I'm on vacation and just happened to pass through town."

"Where do you live now?"

"The company I work for just transferred me from their Phoenix office to Houston seven months ago." Which was her first, entirely truthful answer.

"What's the company—if you don't mind me asking?" the brunette tacked on the qualification as if realizing she might sound nosy.

"No. It's an electronics firm called Data-Corp." It was almost a relief to talk about her work, a totally unemotional subject.

"Electronics." Her dark eyes widened expressively, as if indicating it was out of her league. "That's a growing field."

"It's very challenging work," Angie replied. "And the pay is good, as well as the benefits. I was fortunate to be hired by them straight out of college."

"An Arizona university?"

"Yes," she nodded. "I majored in mathematical science at the University of Arizona."

"Then is this your first trip back since you and your parents moved away?" the teacher inquired. Together, they moved out of the doorway into the roomier space of the hall.

"More or less," Angie hedged on her answer. "My parents were killed in a bus crash in Brazil when I was sixteen. They had gone there on a kind of second honeymoon. After that, I was shuffled back and forth among my relatives until I started college."

"That must have been rough," Lucy Gonzales offered sympathetically.

"Yes, well . . . I made it," she declared on an indrawn breath and glanced back to the open door of the classroom, but she didn't mention the pain and heartache she'd had to endure alone.

"Have you looked up any of your old school friends?" The teacher attempted to change the subject to one she thought would have more pleasant memories.

"Not really—no. Most of them have probably moved away. About the only name I still recognize is Blackwood, but the family has been a permanent part of this area almost as long as 'Big Tree'." Angie referred to the live oak tree at Goose Island State Park, reputed to be two thousand years old.

"It does seem the Blackwood family has been around that long," the young teacher agreed with a laugh. "It's going to continue, too. The heir to the Blackwood holdings is in my class of second graders."

The color drained from Angie's face. She felt her knees grow weak as the statement nearly ripped her apart, but the brunette seemed unaware of the impact of her words.

"I guess I should properly refer to Lindy as an heiress," Lucy Gonzales corrected her previous terminology.

"A girl? Her father is Deke Blackwood?" The inflection of her almost frozen voice made it a question, seeking confirmation.

"Yes—" The teacher planned to say more but she was interrupted by the shrilly loud clammer of a bell ringing overhead. She waited until it had stopped ringing to explain to Angie, "That's the first bell. Classes resume in three minutes. The stampede will start any second now," she declared in half-jest. But it seemed almost a cue to Angie, because within seconds after the young teacher's remark there was a sound of running feet entering the building.

"Mrs. Gonzales! Mrs. Gonzales!" The excited voice of a child called to the teacher.

As Angie started to turn, glimpsing a tow-headed child out of the corner of her eye, the teacher murmured an aside to her, "That's Lindy Blackwood."

For a full minute, Angie could only stare at the child who rushed up to the teacher. A terrible pain was wrenching at her heart and lungs, making it difficult to think or breathe. The little girl's hair was the color and texture of cornsilk, secured by gold barrettes on either side. Her build was very slender and petite, but there was a healthy glow to her complexion. It was the child's eyes, however, that trapped Angie—Deke's eyes—so clear and gray, fringed with soot-black lashes.

"Look what I found, Mrs. Gonzales!" Lindy Blackwood uncurled her fingers from around the object clutched in her hand to show it to her teacher. "It's a fossil rock," she declared, proud of her knowledge.

"So it is," Lucy Gonzales agreed after looking at it.

"I found it all by accident. Wasn't I lucky?" the little girl beamed.

"You certainly were."

Angie's taut muscles loosened enough to allow her to crouch down to the little girl's height. "May I see it, Lindy?" There was a forced lightness to her question.

The girl was proud to show off her find. Angie's fingers trembled as she examined the rock with the fossilized imprint of a leaf that was cradled in the small palm. Angie schooled her expression not to show any of her inner torment when she looked into the gray eyes that so reminded her of Deke.

"That's really something," Angie murmured in feigned admiration for the rock.

The tow-headed child agreed with a vigorous nod, then cocked her head to one side. "How did you know my name?"

"Your teacher told me," Angie explained, rent with anguish and fighting to conceal it.

"Are you a teacher?" The young girl studied Angie with unblinking interest.

"No. I'm just visiting the school." She couldn't meet the directness of that gaze and let her own slide to the rock. "How did you know this was a fossil rock?"

"Because my daddy has one on his desk— only it's bigger and has a scorpion in it instead of a leaf. I'd rather have a leaf," she stated, quite emphatically.

Angie clasped her hands tightly together, struggling to maintain control of her expression. She'd been with Deke when he'd found the rock with the skeletal outline of a scorpion. They'd been out on Mustang Island, looking for sand dollars along the beach—Angie abruptly shut off the memory.

"I like the leaf, too." Her voice was slightly choked, and husky.

The noisy bell sounded again.

"The one-minute warning bell," Lucy Gonzales grimaced.

"I'd better go," Lindy Blackwood sighed, then smiled widely at Angie. "It was nice meeting you." Her mouth went tight as a furrow of concentration puckered her forehead. "I forgot your name. Did you tell me?" she questioned, then smiled ruefully. "Daddy says it's a bad habit to forget people's names, but sometimes a person can't help it," she insisted with pseudo-adultness.

"My name is . . . Angie," she supplied only her given name as Angie became aware of the tide of children flooding the hall.

"'Bye, Angie." The blond-haired girl was quickly engulfed by her classmates and swept into the second grade classroom.

Angie didn't have an opportunity to respond to the wave from Lindy's teacher, busy shepherding her pupils into the room with some degree of orderliness. Angie stared at the point where she'd last seen the child until the final bell rang. Then she moved numbly to the exit, and out the door to her car.

Before she had driven two blocks, her vision became clouded with tears. Angie realized she should never have come to Rockport. It was worse now than before. Ignorance had been better than knowing. She began trembling, shaking from the brutal pain that had become worse instead of better.

A horn blared and brakes squealed. She swerved the car just in time to avoid hitting another. Considering her state of mind, she wasn't fit to be on the road. She pulled into the first motel she found. It wasn't until then that Angie realized she had backtracked. She was only a few blocks away from the very intersection where her journey into the past had begun.

Taking deep, shuddering breaths, she sat behind the wheel for several minutes, then made a half-hearted attempt to wipe the moisture from her cheeks. The face in the rearview mirror looked drained and exhausted, which was precisely the way she felt.

Finally Angie climbed out of the car and walked on shaky legs to the door marked "Office." A bell jingled above the doorway when she entered. An elderly man appeared in the opening to a back room and walked to the reception counter.

"I'd like a room, please." There was a definite waver in her voice, revealing the thin edge of her poise.

"Single or double?" the dour-faced man asked.

"Single."

"How many nights?" He pushed a registration form across the counter for Angie to fill out.

"One." But even as she said it, Angie doubted that she would leave. Not right away.

The situation was so impossible. She couldn't leave and she couldn't stay. Why hadn't she left things the way they were? It had been bearable. But not now.

Her hand was trembling. She had to grip the cheap ballpoint pen hard in order to make her name a legible scrawl. With a strange vagueness, she saw that she had written "Angie Smith" instead of "Hall." Why the subterfuge? What was she hoping to gain? Perhaps time to come to her senses? To use the strong, logical sense of her mind, instead of being controlled by her emotions.

"Will this be cash or credit card?" the elderly clerk questioned.

"Cash." Angie opened her clutch purse to pay him. She had no choice. With a false name on the registry, it was impossible to use one of her credit cards without inviting a lot of questions about her right name, which she didn't want to answer.

After writing out a cash receipt, the clerk handed her a room key and gave her directions on how to find it and where to park her car. Angie was so overwrought that she only remembered half of it and ended up lugging her suitcase the length of one hallway before she found the door with a number that corresponded to the key she'd been given.

Her interest in the clean, sparsely furnished room was nil. She left her suitcase where she'd sat it down on the floor, not bothering to set it on the luggage rack provided. She sank onto the firm mattress, not noticing the bright, cinnamon chenille bedspread covering it. Her thoughts were in turmoil. Right and wrong seemed interchangeable. The only clear delineation in her mind was between the past and the present.

Chapter Two

$\mathcal{T}$ he loud, laughing voices of a family with teenagers walking past her motel room door finally roused Angie to her surroundings. Hardly any light was coming through the window, creating shadows in the room. She switched on the lamp by the bed and glanced at her watch. It was after six. There was a lost sensation that so much time had gone by without her being aware of it. The giddy weakness she felt was obviously caused by hunger. It was suddenly important to have a purpose, even if it was something as basic as eating.

Her purse was on the bed. It took Angie a minute to find the key to the room. Considering how disoriented she had been when she arrived at her motel room, she found the small restaurant attached to the motel with surprising ease. A few patrons were already there, but Angie found a quiet table off by herself and sat down.

Loud music from a jukebox filtered through the door that connected the restaurant to the adjoining bar. The laughter and camaraderie coming from the other side seemed alien to Angie. The world weighed so heavily on her shoulders, a cumbersome yoke of depression pulling her spirits down.

The evening special on the restaurant's menu was red snapper which the waitress recommended very highly. Angie ordered it. The meal was not only tasty, but the nourishment also chased away some of her leadenness. She felt buoyed by it, briefly lifted out of that canyon of despair when she finished her meal.

With that purpose over, the evening stretched emptily ahead of her. It became mandatory not to think after the wasted afternoon when she had thought herself into a daze of confusion. The noise from the bar beckoned to her as Angie went to the cash register to pay for her meal. A coin-operated cigarette machine stood against the wall. Angie added another bill to the money she handed the cashier.

"Some change for cigarettes, please," she requested, even though she'd quit smoking more than four years ago. Tonight Angie wanted the companionship of a cigarette.

With the package of cigarettes and a matchbook in her purse, Angie walked to the connecting door to the bar. Typically, the lighting inside was dim. She had to wait a couple of seconds inside the doorway to give her eyes a chance to adjust to the absence of light.

All the inhabitants seemed to be male, an unusual mixture of cowboys and shrimpers. No one was sitting on the stools at the end of the bar. Angie made her way quietly to the last one. Her appearance didn't go unnoticed. She received more than one interested and appraising look, but her posture and attitude didn't invite any overtures, much to the disappointment of the lookers.

The bartender was a dark-haired man in his late forties, his muscled bulk inclining to go to fat. There was a gruffness to his features and demeanor, but there was an extraordinary gentleness in his eyes when he paused across the counter from where Angie was seated on a tall barstool.

"What'll it be?" He rested his hairy hands on the counter's edge and partially leaned his weight on it.

If she drank any liquor, it was usually white wine. But it seemed inappropriate to order that here. "A beer. Whatever you have on tap." She wasn't particular about brands.

While Angie opened the pack of cigarettes, the bartender tipped a glass under a beer tap and filled it nearly full before setting a head on it. He carried it over and rummaged behind the counter until he found a paper coaster to sit the glass on, then placed it in front of her.

"Don't recall seeing you in here before," he remarked with a faint welcoming smile. "Are you from here?"

"I used to be," Angie admitted and tore a match out of the book before striking it and holding the flame to her cigarette. She almost coughed when she inhaled.

"Back for a visit, huh?" the bartender surmised.

"No." Angie didn't object to company, but she wasn't interested in conversation.

"The area has changed a lot—growing all the time. Tourists in the winter and tourists in the summer," he observed.

"Yes."

The bartender took the hint from her one-syllable replies and wandered to the other end of the bar. Angie tapped her cigarette tip in the ashtray and sipped at the cold beer. She had vowed not to think, but she kept wondering what would happen if she called Marissa and immediately shied away from the prospect. She listened to the music playing on the jukebox, not hearing the lyrics.

One cowboy continued to show an increasing interest in her, studying her with a curiously intent look as if trying to place where he'd seen her before. A toasty brown mustache bushed and curled away from his upper lip. Dressed in Levis and a printed western shirt, he was wearing a spanking new Stetson with a decorative featherband. He stared at Angie until he couldn't contain his curiosity any longer and pushed out of his chair to cross the room.

Angie noticed him when he leaned sideways against the bar facing her stool. There was a suggestion of a smile to his mouth, but the curving line disappeared into the mustache. Coolly ignoring him, she turned away. His blue eyes narrowed in thoughtful, yet confused speculation.

"This is either going to sound like a bad line from an old movie or an old line from a bad movie," he began, "but—don't I know you?"

A little chill ran down her spine. Angie glanced briefly at the cowboy again, seeing something vaguely familiar about his features. "No, I don't think you do," she denied even though she wasn't sure.

"I'm just positive we've met somewhere before," he insisted with a slight shake of his head. "Do you live around here?"

"No." She'd put her cigarette out barely a minute ago, but she was suddenly apprehensive and reached for another.

The snap of a metallic lighter sounded as the cowboy offered her its flame. Angie let him light her cigarette, but avoided contact with his sharp gaze.

"I've done some traveling myself. Where are you from?" he asked.

"Arizona." She curled her hands around the beer glass, studying the smoke swirling from the cigarette between her fingers. She felt wary and on edge.

There was a rueful grimace at her answer. "I've never been there." He paused to study her profile again. "I know we've met before. It's embarrassing to think I could forget those blue eyes or that naturally blond hair." Angie didn't respond to the implied compliment. "I never introduced myself. The name is Kelly. Kelly Reynolds."

His name rippled through her like a miniature shock wave. That was the name she hadn't been able to recall earlier. It belonged to the young man Marissa had been dating that summer seven years ago. Kelly knew her. After seven years, he simply hadn't recognized her—and she hadn't recognized him. Angie struggled to keep her reaction from showing—to conceal that his name meant anything to her.

"Sorry, but I've never heard the name before," she lied, feigning indifference and deliberately failing to tell him her own.

"I'd swear I know you." He continued to scrutinize her, much to Angie's dismay.

She tried to appear nonchalant. "I probably remind you of someone else. It happens." She shrugged.

"Maybe," Kelly sounded skeptical. He slid onto the vacant barstool next to her, not giving up. "To rephrase another bad line, what brings a nice girl like you to this sleepy Texas town? It's a little off the beaten path."

"I'll borrow another old line." The curved line of her mouth was stiff. "I'm just passing through."

"—and just happened to stop here for the night," he concluded with continuing doubt.

"That's hardly so unusual," Angie defended. "I understand this area receives its share of tourists."

"I guess so," Kelly conceded reluctantly. He lit a cigarette of his own and glanced sideways at her through the smoke. "Maybe it was San Antonio that we met."

"I've never been there." Somehow she had to stop this conversation without rousing his suspicions further.

He pursed his lips thoughtfully and motioned to the bartender. "I'll have a beer, Al," he ordered and sent another half-smiling glance at Angie. "Let me buy you a fresh drink."

"No, thanks," she refused. "I've barely touched the one I have." She took another sip, fully aware the beer had become flat.

There was a lull as the bartender brought him a bottle of beer and a glass. Kelly dug the money out of his hip pocket to pay for it. When the bartender went to get his change, the cowboy turned his head to study Angie again.

"What did you say your name was?" he prompted.

This was becoming dangerous. Any minute he might remember her. What if he knew the story? What if he called Deke and told him she was in town? All hell would break loose. Was she ready for that? Or was she willing to resign herself to the status quo? It was a decision Angie hadn't been able to make yet. Soon Kelly Reynolds might force her into a course of action she might not want.

"I didn't tell you my name." Her voice was frozen with icy cold fear.

With an unnatural display of cowardice, Angie gathered the pack of cigarettes and matchbook, shoving them inside her purse. As she slid off the barstool to leave, he grabbed at her arm. Surprise was mixed with confusion in his expression.

"Don't go," Kelly protested.

"It's late and I've had a long day." She firmly extricated herself from his hold. "Good night, Mr. Reynolds."

As she walked to the exit leading into the restaurant, Angie could feel his intent gaze burrowing into her back. Right up to the very last second, he was trying to place when and where he'd known her before. Angie had the feeling that she'd handled the situation badly, whetting his curiosity about her identity instead of diverting it. She should have made up a name, rather than refusing to tell him. Now it was too late. She was angry with herself— angry and a little scared.

When the door closed behind her, Kelly Reynolds turned back to the bar and folded his arms across its top. His heavy sigh betrayed his inner confused and troubled state. The bartender paused, eyeing him thoughtfully and with a trace of amusement.

"Strike out, did ya', Kelly?" he mocked.

"Naw." Kelly picked up the bottle of beer and poured its liquid into the glass. His expression remained contemplative. "I've met that blond somewhere before. Dammit, I know I have." There was more than a trace of frustration in his voice.

"You probably have," the bartender shrugged as he removed the partially empty glass of beer Angie had left. "She told me she used to live around here."

"She lived here?" Kelly repeated on a surprised note, because she had denied it to him. "But—" He stopped in the middle of a half-formed protest. "Did she say when?"

"No. But I had the impression it was a few years ago." He looked at Kelly and smiled dryly. "I never realized there had been so many blonds in your life that you wouldn't remember a number like that one."

"That's what bugs me," Kelly admitted on a disgruntled note. "I haven't dated that many."

"Maybe you didn't date this one," the bartender suggested. "It could be that she wouldn't give you the time of day even back then."

There was a moment of silence as Kelly studied the foamy top of his beer. Slowly he lifted his head, a dawning light glimmering in his eyes.

"That's it," he murmured. "She was dating someone else." He snapped his fingers in sudden recall. "Deke. It was Deke. I was taking

Marissa out then and we used to double with Deke and that blond. Damn." He bit at his lower lip. "What was her name?" He muttered the question to himself. "Mandy? No. Tammy? No."

"When was this?" Now the bartender was curious.

"It was a little before Deke ran off and got married," Kelly replied absently. "I wish I could remember her name. It's going to drive me crazy until I think of it."

The bartender's train of thought traveled in a different direction, focusing on Deke Blackwood. "Ya' know, I can't help feeling sorry for Blackwood. The man's sure had his share of grief, first losing his bride when she gave premature birth to his daughter, then his father getting killed in the crash of a light plane, and his mother passing away two years ago. I guess that goes to prove that there's some things money can't buy."

"I tell ya', I'd give a hundred dollars if I could remember that blond's name," Kelly declared.

"It won't cost a hundred dollars," the bartender replied cryptically. "Just the price of a phone call."

It took a second for the cowboy to follow his thinking. "You're right!" Kelly scooped up the small change on the countertop. "Either Deke or Marissa will be home. I'll just call and ask."

He stepped off the barstool and headed toward the pay telephone in the back hall by the rest rooms.

The walls in the den were cream-colored, giving the room an open, spacious feeling. A walnut gun cabinet stood near the door to the foyer, gleaming rifle barrels showing through its locked, glass door. Another area of the room was occupied by two overstuffed armchairs covered in roughly grained brown leather, worn smooth with age and usage. On the floor in front of the matching chairs was a large, woven mat, geometric designs stained into it with natural dyes. A massive desk dominated the room. A century old, its pecan wood was accented with heavy brass trappings.

Seated in the desk's companion chair, Deke Blackwood made the day's entries in the ledger opened before him. Having played in the den as a child, he was unimpressed by the aura of authority and power that was in the air.

The responsibility that went along with the right to occupy the chair behind the desk had long ago wiped away the carefreeness of youth from his face. At thirty-two, he bore the stamp of experienced command. His hardened features were marked with lines of cynicism that seemed to look upon the world with weary humor. Handsome was no longer a word that described him, although all the ingredients were there—dark hair, the color of bronze—gray eyes with the sheen of polished steel—

and a rangy muscled build. He was like a wolf who had learned to survive by his wits and cunning, and no longer relied on mere good looks. In some intangible way, that altered his appearance.

A faint sound broke his concentration. His senses were trained to be ever on the alert. They became centered, now, on discovering the source of the sound—the whisper of soft material coming from the open door. Deke lifted his gaze from the column of figures and let it glide to the door. A young blond-haired girl was peering cautiously into the room, her look expectant and hopeful, one bare foot resting atop its mate. His mouth crooked in a half-smile at the sight of his daughter, but the fiercely possessive love in his eyes was more reflective of his true reaction. His glance skimmed her, taking note of the lavender nightgown and matching cotton robe.

"Is it that late already?" Deke glanced at his watch as he closed his ledger book for the time being. His action was the indication Lindy Blackwood had been waiting for as she scampered into the room, darting around the desk to his chair. "I guess it is eight o'clock," he acknowledged what his watch had revealed. He pivoted the swivel chair at right angles to the desk and lifted the child onto his knee.

"Are you through with your work?" Lindy asked with a glance at the closed account book.

"Not quite." Deke studied his daughter with

an absolute pleasure. Lindy was the shining light in his life, practically the only one still left. He was highly protective of her, motivated by a certain selfishness. It was evident when he curved an arm around her small shoulders and snuggled her close to him. Bending his head, Deke brushed his mouth across the silkenness of her platinum hair. "Mmm. You smell good."

"Aunt Marissa let me put some of her perfume in my bath water." She gave him a sidelong look, precociously testing her flirting skills. Little girls always tried them out on their own daddies first. For the time being, it amused him, but Deke wasn't sure how he'd feel when she got older and turned her charms on some young man.

"You're too anxious to grow up," Deke murmured, because he knew how many ways she could be hurt.

But Lindy paid no attention to his remark. "My rock looks nice sitting on the desk next to yours." She drew his glance to the large fossilized stone that acted as a paperweight and the little one sitting in its shadow.

"It certainly does," Deke agreed.

"I thought I was lucky to find it, but Mrs. Gonzales said that I had sharp eyes," Lindy repeated the praise from her teacher. "Angie asked me how I knew what it was and I told her about your rock."

The name vibrated through him. It was a slight shock to hear it spoken by his daughter. "Who is Angie? One of your classmates?"

"No. Angie is the lady who was visiting Mrs. Gonzales at school today," Lindy explained blithely. "When I brought my rock in to show my teacher, she asked to see it. She thought I was clever for remembering about yours."

"That was clever," Deke echoed the praise.

"Tomorrow I'm going to look for some more," she stated.

"Speaking of tomorrow, it's time you were getting to bed." As he started to slide her off his lap, the telephone rang. After a second's hesitation, he set her down. "Run along to bed," Deke instructed while reaching to pick up the phone. "I'll be there in a few minutes to tuck you in."

Obediently, Lindy did as she was told. Deke watched her go, lifting the telephone receiver to silence its shrill ring, but not carrying it to his ear until his daughter had disappeared. The swivel chair squeaked as he leaned back in it.

"Blackwood." He spoke into the mouthpiece.

"Deke? Kelly Reynolds," the male voice on the other end of the phone identified himself.

Mild surprise registered in Deke's expression. "Hello, Kelly. How've you been?"

"Fine." It was a quick reply, dismissing the pleasantries. "What I was calling about, Deke —Do you remember that blond you dated a few years back? She spent the summer here visiting some relative."

Deke stiffened, his blood running cold for an

instant. "Angie?" Harshness made it an accusing question.

"Angie! That's it!" Kelly exclaimed in satisfaction.

Deke leaned forward in his chair, his features growing hard. "What about her?" he demanded.

"She was here at Al's, having a drink. I finally recognized her, but I couldn't remember her name. I knew I would go crazy until I found out what it was, that's why I called you." He laughed shortly in mixed relief. "Now I can have some peace."

A white-hot rage began to thaw the coldness that had momentarily gripped Deke. A deadly quiet entered his voice. "Did she say what she was doing in town?"

"Just passing through, she said," Kelly replied indifferently. "I guess she's spending the night here at the motel." A muscle leaped along Deke's jawline. "Well, I won't keep ya', Deke. Give Marissa my regards."

"Yes." It was an absent response, a galling bitterness filling his thoughts.

The line went dead. Deke replaced the telephone receiver on its cradle, visibly struggling to control the surge of raw anger that swept through him. Nearly possessed by it, he pushed out of his chair and circled the desk, crossing the room with long strides.

In the foyer, he paused to drag his naturally tanned leather jacket from the halltree and clamp a charcoal black Stetson atop his head.

As he shrugged into the tailored jacket, footsteps approached the foyer. His steel gaze thrust itself into his dark-haired sister when she appeared. Her glance was startled.

"Where are you going?" Marissa frowned in confusion. "Lindy's waiting for you to tell her good night."

"I have to go to town." His answer was brisk, too severely controlled.

There was trouble in the air. Marissa could almost hear the crackling of electricity in the room. Something was very wrong or Deke wouldn't be leaving without tucking Lindy into bed. But he was leaving—going into town, he said—without explanation.

"Why?" she blurted the demand and watched him pause, his hand on the doorknob. His gray eyes were cold and emotionless when they met her searching look. Yet she had the curious sensation of being burned as if a wild fire raged behind them.

"Have there been any calls today that you failed to mention to me?" There was a hint of derision in his tone, a vague accusation that she had been deliberately keeping something from him.

Despite the surface appearance of devotion, she and her brother had never been close—not in the sense that they confided in each other or shared their deepest thoughts. Marissa loved her brother and would have welcomed a relationship like that, but Deke kept his own council, never allowing her to get too close. Marissa understood because he'd lost so many people that he cared about. If it wasn't for Lindy, she would have believed that he'd lost the capacity to care about another human being. Their personalities had become very divergent. More than once Deke had accused her of being too soft-hearted and gullible. Such things hurt, just as his veiled challenge that she had deliberately kept something important from him now.

"No one called other than those on the list I left on your desk," Marissa insisted.

"No one?" His low drawl was almost taunting. "Not even Angie?"

Shock wiped the color from her face, a reaction Deke's sharp gaze was quick to note. It was impossible for his sister to hide her feelings. He was almost irritated with himself for doubting her loyalty, except he knew her feelings could be manipulated. And Angie was an expert at that.

"Angie," Marissa whispered the name. "Has she . . . ?" She stopped before finishing the question.

Deke already knew what it was going to be. "Yes. Kelly says she's in town."

"And that's where you're going?" she breathed.

"Yes. I want to find out what's on her cold, little mind." A thick thread of embittered anger ran through his voice. "If it's trouble she wants, I'll give her all she can handle."

"Deke—" Her voice seemed to plead with him not to be hasty, but he was already walking out the door.

Chapter Three

By the time Angie reached her motel room, she was in a confused state of indecision. She was usually a very decisive person, fully aware of what she wanted and how to obtain it—in control of her emotions at all times. At least, that's what she had always believed about herself. Except for that one lapse with Deke, although, of course, there had been extenuating circumstances. She had been with Deke too soon after the death of her parents. She had been grasping for something to fill the void. Luckily she had come to her senses in time.

Or had she? Angie paced about the small room. She was shaking, a mass of trembling nerves. Why hadn't she been able to forget? Why hadn't she put the past behind her? If she was so convinced she had done the right thing, why had the memory of it lurked at the back of her every waking moment?

Angie stopped asking herself why she had come back. She knew it was because she hadn't been able to forget. But what was she to do now that she was here? She couldn't walk away again as she had done before, supposedly with a clear conscience. It had never been clear, she realized that now.

A sensation of pain, more physical than mental, intruded on her thinking. Angie glanced at her hands. They were twisted so tightly together that little circulation was reaching her fingers. Her nerves were shot. She halted by the bedside table and unclasped her hands to open her purse. Shaking a cigarette out of the pack, Angie lit it to give her trembling hand something else to hold.

No longer able to trust the wisdom of her own counsel, she wished for someone to talk to, someone who could give her advice. But who could she call? Who could she trust? Her anxious gaze ran to the phone on the table next to the bed.

There was one person who had taken an active interest in her of late. Angie hadn't discouraged it, although she hadn't allowed herself to become emotionally involved. She hesitated, then crushed out the half-smoked cigarette in the ashtray and reached for the phone. Angie dialed the number without conscious thought. She'd always had a natural facility for remembering telephone numbers.

The motel switchboard came on the line, and Angie gave her room number, then listened to the ringing of the phone on the other end. On the fourth ring, it was answered.

"Hello, Ted?" Angie heard the stress in her voice. "It's Angie."

Ted Sullivan was in charge of the legal department in the Houston branch of Data-Corp. A young, aggressive man, he was one of the first people she'd met after being transferred. It was an advantage Ted had quickly followed up by setting himself up to be her personal guide to the city. Angie had enjoyed his company, finding him both intelligent and amusing. So far, he hadn't demanded more from her than she had been willing to give.

"Angie! I didn't expect you to call tonight!" But his delight was evident. "How's Corpus Christi?"

"I don't know. I didn't make it that far." She tried to make it a joke, but her voice sounded very brittle and strained.

There was a slight pause before Ted spoke, his interest sharpened. "What happened? Did you have car trouble?"

"No. Nothing like that." Angie hesitated because she didn't know how to lead the conversation around to the topic she wanted to discuss. She began to question why she'd called him in the first place.

"Where are you?" It was not a completely idle question. He seemed to sense that all was not well.

"Rockport," she admitted. "It's just north of

48

Corpus Christi on the Gulf. I made it this far and decided to stop."

"What's in Rockport?"

Angie could have told him but she stalled the moment of truth. "An aunt of mine lived here a few years ago. I remembered visiting her one summer and . . . thought I'd look around."

"You never mentioned you had any relation in Texas," Ted said with some surprise.

"I don't—not anymore." It was a quick lie. She was suddenly frightened, wondering if she had called him to seek personal advice— or professional? Angie reached for another cigarette to soothe her shattered nerves.

"What was that?" Ted demanded.

"What?" Angie frowned at the question.

"The noise on the phone."

"That was me." She realized she had been holding the matchbook next to the receiver's mouthpiece when she struck the match to light her cigarette. "I was just lighting a cigarette."

There was another pause before Ted replied in a troubled voice, "I've never seen you smoke."

"I don't as a rule—just every now and then." That sounded feeble.

"Angie, what's wrong?" he questioned with concern. "Something's bothering you. I can hear it in your voice."

"That's nonsense." She heard herself deny it and realized that she wasn't going to be able to confide in him.

"No, it isn't," Ted refused to believe her. "You're upset. I can tell. Why did you call me, Angie?"

"I didn't really have a reason," she lied. "I just thought I'd let you know about my change of plans." But that was out of character, too. It indicated that their relationship was a close one, otherwise she wouldn't feel the need to account for where she was. They were on very friendly terms, but certainly not intimate.

"What's this?" There was a smile in his tone, as well as some confusion. "Has 'absence made the heart grow fonder'?"

It seemed easier to agree than to be cross-examined. "Maybe so."

"That's encouraging." Ted sounded pleased. "How long are you planning to stay in Rockport?"

"I'm not sure." She groped for a more definite answer, agitated and on edge. "Maybe for a couple more days. It depends."

There was another pause. "Are you sure you're all right, Angie? You don't sound like yourself."

"I'm fine. Really," she insisted, but she felt close to tears. Her voice was threatening to break. "I'd better let you go, Ted."

"I'm glad you called, Angie," he said and meant it.

"Yes," she murmured. "Bye."

Before he could say anything to detain her, Angie hung up the phone breaking the connection. It had been wrong to try to involve someone else in her problems. They were hers to solve—no one else's. So what did she intend to do about them? She had always been so realistic. What did she want to do? She rubbed her forehead, trying to silence the pounding.

A hard rap on the door seemed to explode inside her head. With a burst of impatience, Angie sprang to her feet and stalked to the door. She didn't think to use the security chain as she yanked the door open.

All motion ceased the instant she saw Deke standing outside. The intervening years since she'd last seen him had hardened his male features into implacable lines. The curve of his cheekbone was harsh; his jaw unyielding. He seemed bigger than she remembered—not so much taller as broader. His chest and shoulders had muscled out, although there was still the leanness of a predatory beast about him. The brim of his hat shadowed his eyes, giving him a hooded look. Angie caught their glitter, but it wasn't the silver brilliance that used to excite her. When he took a step forward, she saw they held the glitter of polished steel, sharp and cutting.

Paralysis gripped her throat, preventing her from speaking. Her hand was holding the door ajar. The flat of his hand pushed it the rest of the way open as Deke walked in, uninvited, and Angie hastily backed out of his way. He closed it behind him with a deliberateness that started her pulse racing. His gaze never left her, not for a second. He despised her. Angie could see it in his eyes, and inwardly cringed.

"How—" Her voice cracked on the attempted question and she stopped to gather her wits and her courage.

"Kelly." The corners of his mouth lifted in a nasty imitation of a smile. A certain dullness crept into her senses. The flatness of his voice reminded her of a cracking whip. "He recognized you and called out to the ranch when he couldn't remember your name."

It was exactly what she had feared. She lowered her chin, turning her head slightly away from him to avoid the condemnation of his eyes. How would she ever make him understand? It seemed totally hopeless.

"You were at the school today, too, weren't you?" Deke accused in the same deadly flat tone.

All Angie could do was nod her head slightly in silent admission. If there had been any hint of gentleness or compassion in his expression, she would have thrown herself into his arms and cried out her anguish. But there was none.

"Why the hell are you here, Angie?" The air around her seemed to seethe with the contained fury in his demand.

It snapped her chin up and brought her gaze back to him. Meekness was alien to her nature. Defiance shimmered in her blue eyes. "You know why I came back, Deke."

"You have no right to be here," he reminded her brutally. "You gave it up almost seven years ago."

"Maybe I have no legal right," she conceded

52

as hot tears of anger and pain rose in her eyes. "But she's still my child, too!"

"Lindy is *my* daughter." There was no mistaking the emphasis of possession. "You didn't want her. You didn't even want to know whether you gave birth to a boy or a girl!"

Angie stiffened at his deliberately cruel reminder. "Why do you think I'm here?" she retaliated. "I couldn't stand not knowing. I tried to forget! I tried to pretend that I didn't care! But I had to find out. I wanted to see my baby!"

"Do you expect me to believe that?" Deke jeered. "You never displayed any curiosity before now. Not in seven years."

"How do you know?" she flared. "How do you know what I've thought or felt all this time?" She was losing her temper fast, giving into the storm of emotions that raged within her. Pivoting, she took a couple of quick steps to put some distance between them before she gave into the childish temptation to assault him physically. She stopped in front of the chest of drawers, grabbing hold of its carved edge. "You don't know anything about what I've been thinking and feeling all these years —wondering if my baby is healthy or—"

"You can stop wondering," Deke inserted harshly. "She's fine, if you ever really cared."

She whirled to glare at him. "I care. That's a rotten thing to say, Deke Blackwood," she accused huskily. "I cared enough to make certain she had a good home and someone to love her. What could I have given her? I was only seventeen! I didn't have the means to take care of myself, let alone a baby! How could I have gotten an education, worked and raised a child, too? I had no choice!" Angie cried. "I had to give her up."

His jaw hardened into a cold line, his mouth thinning. "You had a choice. I gave you one."

She looked away. "Yes, you did. Marriage." Bitterness laced her words. "That convinced me quicker than anything that I wasn't ready to be a parent. It was bad enough being a seventeen-year-old bride. But don't worry—" she laughed shortly and harshly, "—no one can ever say that a Blackwood didn't do the honorable thing. It was a mistake from the start and you know it."

"Yes." His voice was once again flat. "You made your feelings about our marriage very clear. And your feelings for our child."

Facing him again, Angie made an appeal for his understanding. "Do you think it was an easy decision to give up my baby? Why do you think I insisted on not being told whether it was a boy or a girl? Why do you think I refused to see it?" No emotion was revealed by his hard, masculine features, nothing to indicate her anguished voice was touching him. "I knew," Angie continued, choking a little, "I knew if I saw it—if I held my baby, I'd never be able to let it go!"

"I'm not particularly interested in the past, Angie." Deke wasn't moved by her confession. "All that matters is that you relinquished all claims to your daughter and gave me absolute custody."

"But that doesn't change the fact that I'm her mother," she argued.

"You *were* her mother." He stressed the past tense.

"I still am," Angie insisted. "A piece of paper doesn't change that. Any more than it could change that you are Lindy's father."

"I'm glad you recognize that I am her father," he stated grimly.

"I never denied it," she retorted. "And I never blamed you for getting me pregnant either. It was equally my fault. I knew what I was doing." She turned back to the chest of drawers, her eyes closing to allow images of that summer to flash through her mind. "I was so lonely." Her voice was barely above a whisper. "I'd just lost my parents and I was desperate for someone to love. You came along at a time when I needed someone—someone to show me a little affection. I wanted to belong to someone—anyone. I often think that it didn't matter who."

For awhile, it had been absolute bliss. Then she had discovered she was pregnant. She was seventeen and terrified. Morning sickness had made it impossible to hide her condition from her aunt. Even after all this time, Angie could still remember the awful humiliation she'd gone through when her aunt had summoned Deke and his parents to her house. For the sake of the Blackwood family name and the legitimacy of the unborn child, it was understood that Deke would naturally marry her. But he had suddenly seemed like a stranger to her.

The day after his parents and her aunt agreed the young couple would marry, Angie had boarded a bus and ran away to an uncle in Phoenix. Unbeknownst to her, he called her aunt when she arrived at his home. The next thing she knew Deke and his parents showed up at her uncle's. Family pressure forced her into marrying him, but she couldn't stop herself from seeing a stranger each time she looked at him. She wasn't frightened of him; it was simply that she didn't know him except in the most intimate sense. How could she spend the rest of her life with a man she didn't even know if she liked?

When she refused to return to Texas with him, Deke had agreed to get an apartment in Phoenix. They were to stay there until after the baby was born. While he looked for a suitable one, Angie continued to live with her uncle and his family. Eventually, Deke had realized that she was never going to like any apartment he showed her since it meant living with him.

They quarreled, but Angie rebelled at the thought of living with a stranger as his wife. More than that, she began to realize that she couldn't raise the baby by herself. There was so much more she wanted to do with her life. Without a high school education, she didn't have a chance of obtaining a job to earn enough for herself and a baby. And she'd always dreamed of going on to college which was out of the question.

If she'd simply been an unwed mother, she could have given her baby up for adoption. But she was married. A month before the baby was born, Angie had confronted Deke with her proposition. He would give her an annulment, after all, he had only married her out of a sense of duty. And she would give him custody of their unborn baby. It hadn't been an easy decision, but she was confident that her baby would have a loving home. Deke's parents had been anxious for their first grandchild, showering Angie with baby gifts in eager anticipation.

She had thought it all through. Her decision had been the only logical, sensible, practical one she could reach. Deke had accepted her offer and walked out. Angie hadn't seen him again until she went to the hospital. He'd come into her room after the baby was born and asked her if she wanted to change her mind. When she said 'no,' he'd produced papers for her to sign with a nurse as a witness. Deke hadn't said another word to her and walked out of the room—and her life. She had cried for a week.

The tears had eventually stopped, but not the torment—the torment of knowing she'd given birth to a child. She had thought she would get over it, but she'd never stopped thinking about her baby. She had never stopped thinking and wondering. Had it been a son or a daughter? Was it well? Was it happy?

Just thinking it all through again gave Angie a measure of release. There was less tension in her expression when she turned to look at Deke. He was quietly studying her. She softened at the absence of hostility in his eyes.

"Don't you see, Deke?" Angie reasoned. "I had to come. I had to see Lindy." She wanted to tell him how exciting it was just to know the name of her child. "I had to know she was happy and healthy."

But his look became hard and measuring. "You've seen her. She's doing just fine. you accomplished what you set out to do." There was a slight pause. "What time are you leaving in the morning?"

Angie caught her lower lip between her teeth and turned back to the chest of drawers. She stared at her hands, holding onto the carved ledge around it.

"I'm not leaving, Deke," she replied quietly.

"Like hell you're not." His low voice broke over her like distant thunder, threatening and angry. In the next second, his hand was gripping her upper arm in a talon-hard hold and swinging her around to face him. He caught the other arm in a matching grip.

"I can't go, Deke," Angie exhorted him to understand. "I thought I could. I thought if I saw her, it would be enough, but it isn't. I want to see her again—all the time. I want her back, Deke."

His fingers bit into her flesh, cutting off the circulation. "Do you think you can walk back into her life as easily as you walked out of it?" he charged. "Do you honestly believe I would allow it?"

"Is it asking so much to let me see her sometimes? You've had her all to yourself all this time," she appealed. "Can't you share her with me now?"

His hands tightened for a fraction of a second before Deke pushed her away from him as if he was revolted by the physical contact with her. "No."

As he started to walk away, Angie realized he was intending to leave. She ran after him, catching him by the arm, but he shrugged her off. She finally pushed in front of him to block the way, pressing her back against the closed door.

"Why can't you listen to me?" she demanded indignantly, angered by the way he was autocratically brushing aside her pleas.

"I've listened to you," he returned evenly. "You should have considered this possibility when you gave up all rights to your daughter. Now you want them back, or at least partially. I suppose you expect me to feel sorry for you. Well, I don't."

"What about Lindy?" Angie retorted, stung by his complete lack of sympathy. "Don't you think she needs a mother's love?"

"Lindy is a happy, well-adjusted child. As far as she's concerned, and everyone else in town, her mother is dead. It seemed kinder than telling her that her mother simply didn't want her."

"I—" Angie attempted to protest.

"Can you imagine how confused she'd be if I brought you home and said, 'Lindy, this is your mother. I guess she didn't die after all.'" Deke mocked, but there was a very definite logic.

Angie relented slightly. "It isn't necessary for you to tell her who I am. You could introduce me as a distant relative. Deke, I only want to be with her—to have her spend an afternoon or a day with me now and again," she pleaded.

"For how long?" He eyed her coldly. "How long before you got tired of playing mother? Suppose Lindy grows to love you and a few months down the road, you leave and simply forget to come back. Do you think she'll understand if seven years go by before she sees you again?" His challenge was coolly sarcastic, meant to hurt.

"That won't happen," Angie stated.

"It will. That's your pattern." His gaze ran over her face, taking in the delicate features and missing their underlying strengths. "I'm not going to let you hurt Lindy. You use people, Angie. You use them and toss them aside when the grass looks greener somewhere else. That isn't going to happen to my daughter."

"You're wrong," she protested. "I'm not like that at all." But Angie could tell by his cynical look that he wasn't convinced. It became imperative that she make him understand. She took a step toward him, her hands coming up in a gesture of earnestness. "I've grown up, Deke. Wanting to know my own daughter isn't a passing fad to me." Unconsciously she curved her fingers over the leather lapels of his jacket. His gray eyes were wary, studying her closely. "It isn't easy for me to admit that I made a mistake in giving her up, but I thought I could handle it. I thought the pain would eventually go away. But she's a part of me. I'll always want to be with her—the same as you do."

Her head was tipped back so she could look fully into his eyes and see if her words were making any impression on him at all. Something flickered in iron depths. For a second, Angie thought she had finally reached him. Then his glance drifted to the parted curve of her lips.

A potent sensation of *déjà vu* washed through her and she swayed slightly under its dizzying effect. His hands moved to rest on the soft points of her hipbones, lightly holding her. This had all happened before, so many times that she couldn't recall the number. It was a repetitive pattern with its own set of signals.

Seeing Deke again, it had never occurred to Angie that the sexual attraction they had once known would still exist. But it did. She could still remember the intimate signals that silently invited a kiss or an embrace. The little tilt of her head that would bring his mouth down to hers. She was shaken by the discovery that her body was doing them without the conscious direction of her mind.

The faint lift of a dark eyebrow revealed that Deke noticed it, too. His gaze took on a lazy, sensual quality. Angie was suddenly and vividly aware of his forceful virility. His breath was warm and faintly moist against her sensitive skin, the brutish fragrance of his shaven cheeks stimulated her senses.

"You're feeling it, too, aren't you?" His low voice was husky with disturbed desire.

"Yes," Angie admitted because she didn't really understand it.

But she wasn't given a chance to discuss it as hard, masculine lips covered hers. Their rough demand ignited an immediate spark of pent-up longing. Following habits ingrained long ago, she arched toward him. His hands glided over her spine to bring her more fully against him, her breasts flattening out on contact with the unyielding solidness of his chest. Beneath her fingers, Angie could feel the corded muscles of his neck, dark hair curling over her hands at the back of his head.

The shadow cast by his hat seemed to hide them, letting the embrace become a stolen moment that neither would have to pay for. His mouth moved hungrily over hers, parting its softness and plummeting its secrets. Angie strained closer, afire with an aching fever that made her skin hot to the touch. She was fully conscious of the powerful muscles of his thighs and the hard male outline burning against her. Yet, this was not like any of the other times, something was different, more disturbing by its very familiarity.

She was quivering inside when Deke dragged his mouth to the far corner of her lips. There was a roughness to his breathing and it excited her to know she had aroused him. Angie didn't understand her reaction. There was an odd mixture of regret and relief when Deke pulled away from her. His hands framed her face and raised it for his inspection.

The look in his eyes shocked her. Instead of seeing desire for her written in them, Angie read the message of bitter loathing and died a little. His hands tightened as if he wanted to crush her skull.

"There was a time, Angie, when I would have ripped the moon out of the sky and given it to you on a platter," he growled thickly. "But that was long ago. Now, I don't give a damn."

His complete lack of feelings for her was a shattering discovery, although precisely why, she wasn't sure. Deke pushed her out of the way and opened the door. He paused halfway out and looked over his shoulder.

"Don't try to see Lindy again." There was an implied threat in the warning.

Voiceless, she could only stare. The door was closed with a very definite finality, just as if she was being shut out of his life—and Lindy's. For a frozen moment, she could only stand there. Finally, she turned away from the door.

Her glance strayed around the small hotel room, so impersonal and empty—exactly like her life. It belonged to no one and no one belonged to it. The loneliness of it was almost more than Angie could stand.

In the face of that, Deke's threat didn't seem so intimidating. Lindy was her daughter as much as she was Deke's. She was all Angie had in the world. Now, she knew that she'd never be able to go through the rest of her life without seeing Lindy again. If it meant fighting Deke to do it, then she would fight him tooth and claw. She wasn't going to be separated from Lindy again.

There was no more indecision, and Angie was suddenly exhausted. Turning to the bed, she undressed and pulled back the bedsheets. She crawled naked between them and collapsed. Tomorrow was soon enough to work out the details of her life.

Despite her tiredness, she slept fitfully, never fully resting.

Chapter Four

The next morning, Angie woke up with a dull headache and the feeling that she'd slept for barely an hour, but the sun blazed through the window so she knew it was morning. She dragged herself out of bed and into the bathroom. The stinging spray of the shower revived her, but she still felt emotionally drained by the events of the previous day.

In the restaurant, she lingered over several cups of coffee, trying to decide on a course of action. She had a two-week paid vacation and most of that time left. That gave her plenty of time to see what work was available in the area. Plus she had managed to save a little money, enough to rent a small house or apartment locally.

Before going back to her room, Angie stopped at the motel office to reserve the room for at least two more nights. The same dour-faced man was on duty at the desk. He didn't look pleased to see her when she walked up.

"Checking out?" He held out his hand as if expecting her to give him the room key.

"What?" Angie frowned, disbelief flickering across her face.

"We're all booked up," he repeated his previous assertion. "You said you'd only be wantin' the room for one night, otherwise, I would have told you."

"I see," she murmured and partially turned away from the registration desk. There were other motels so it wasn't really that bad. It was just that she would have to take the time to pack and load her suitcase in the car and she'd been hoping to get to the school while Lindy was on her lunch-break.

"It's nothing personal, you understand," the clerk asserted.

"I understand," Angie sighed.

Returning to her room, she began gathering up her clothes and toiletries that she'd managed to scatter around in a short time. She was just closing the lid on her suitcase when the maid knocked at the door. Angie let her in, then hefted the suitcase off the rack.

"Are you checking out?" the maid inquired with a glance at the suitcase.

"Yes," Angie admitted absently. "I hadn't realized it was so busy here at this time of year."

"Busy?"

"Yes." Angie looked at the woman, a half-formed suspicion suddenly rearing its head again. "I was told the motel was all booked up for the night."

"All booked up? Ha!" It was a derisive laugh. "I've been cleaning here for four years. This place has never been full, except over the holidays."

"I think I knew that," Angie murmured and moved toward the door. Over her shoulder, she said, "Have a nice day."

"Yeah," came the doubting response.

Angie had half a notion to go back to the office and confront the desk clerk with her suspicion. It wasn't the motel that was all booked up. It was simply a fact that there wasn't a room for her. It didn't take too much intelligence to figure out that Deke Blackwood was directly involved in that decision. She should have guessed that he would do something like this. More than likely, he wanted her to know that he was responsible so she wouldn't have any doubts that he wanted her gone.

Her mouth was set in a determined line as she crossed the parking lot to her car. No doubt, the other motels wouldn't have a vacancy either. Deke didn't know her very well if he thought that was going to stand in her way.

She was almost to her car before she noticed the man lounging beside it. Her step faltered as she recognized Deke. His hard gaze touched her, then flicked to the suitcase she carried. His mouth curved, but she didn't mistake the action for a smile.

"Are you leaving?" It was a mocking question.

"You made sure of that, didn't you?" Angie countered without any show of anger. It was oddly difficult to meet his level gaze. In daylight, with all this space around her, Deke seemed more formidable. The suede vest lined with sheepskin added bulk to his wide shoulders and his long, muscled legs were encased in rough denim. Deke wasn't wearing the dark charcoal Stetson he'd had on last night. The brown hat shading his face was faded and work-stained, circled by a band of rattlesnake skin. The years had whipped the softness of youth from him and smoothed the hard surfaces to expose a full-grown man. There was no latent sexuality about him; he was too ruggedly male. Nothing could lessen the impact he made on her senses. Angie was unnerved by it.

She set her suitcase on the ground at the rear of the car and opened her purse for the keys to open the trunk. In her side vision, she was aware of Deke pushing away from the pickup parked next to her car, all in a leisurely flow of motion. His unhurried strides brought him to the rear of the car as she unlocked the trunk.

"I knew you'd be clever enough to figure out it wasn't simple misfortune the motel was booked up for tonight," Deke stated and reached down to pick up her suitcase and set it in the opened trunk.

"But, just in case, you came by so I would be sure to get the message," Angie guessed, but her glance ricocheted away before it fully met the measuring force of his.

"Something like that," he agreed on a lazily cool note. He pushed the trunk closed and paused to lean on it, his head turning to face her squarely. "I don't suppose it will come as any surprise to you to learn there isn't another vacancy in town."

Angie resisted the urge to curl her fingers into fists and forced her expression to remain calm. "You've been busy this morning, haven't you?" The key ring in her hand jingled as she walked to the door on the driver's side, aware that Deke followed at his own unhurried pace. "Are you sure you don't want to escort me out of town as well?"

"I don't think that will be necessary." His hand was there, holding the car door open as Angie slid behind the wheel.

"I'm surprised." Outguessed and thwarted, she was irritated, more so because Deke knew it. She reached out to pull the door shut, but he closed it for her.

The car had sat all morning in the sun and it was hot and stuffy inside. Angie rolled down the window before she inserted the key in the ignition. She didn't have to look to know that Deke was standing by the driver's door. The motor turned over, then hummed steadily. She shifted the gear into reverse and half-turned to look behind her.

"By the way—" Deke's voice came from the window, startling her. Angie turned back and found him bent down to look inside, his large hands resting on the frame of the open window. There was a hard look of satisfaction in his cool gray eyes. "—Lindy isn't in school today. I'm keeping her home for awhile."

His statement struck low and hard, choking her off in mid-breath. All her nerve ends screamed in protest as she stared at him in broken despair. The dark indigo of her eyes pleaded with him to show a little compassion.

"For . . . how long?" Her voice was incredibly hoarse.

There was no give in him. "For as long as it takes."

Hopeless tears welled in her eyes as she swallowed the raw sob that rose in her hot, aching throat. Averting her face, Angie reversed the car out of the parking space without bothering to see if Deke had moved clear or whether any traffic was coming. She didn't doubt for a minute that he would keep Lindy a virtual prisoner on the ranch, certain that, in time, Angie would give up. But he was wrong —he was so wrong to think she would tire of waiting for a chance to see her daughter.

Fighting the waves of despondency, Angie drove out of town without direction. Her plans were smashed and she had to make new ones.

She paid scant attention to the Texas landscape rushing by the car's windows. The highway sliced through coastal marsh lands, giving occasional glimpses of blue Gulf water. In the roadside ditches, herons stood one-legged, poised in their stalk for food, sometimes taking flight in a flap of wings. Windbreaks of brightly flowered oleander bushes dipped and bowed in the draft-generated winds of the traffic.

Angie drove south, seeing none of it. Her mind worked feverishly to find an alternative place to stay now that Deke had eliminated Rockport and Fultan. Aransas Pass and Port Aransas were too obvious; so were Refugio, Gregory and Portland. As she neared Corpus Christi, the sweeping arch of the High Bridge curved into the sky ahead of her. When she crossed it, tugs were guiding an oil tanker under the bridge to the deep-water port and the refineries. Angie had a spectacular view of the bay and the famous shoreline of Corpus Christi with its yacht basin crowded with pleasure craft. But it wasn't the beauty she was observing. It was the hotels and motels that lined the scenic bay drive. The city was big—big enough for her to get lost in—big enough to make it difficult for Deke to find her. She turned off the highway at the next exit.

It was the logical place. A full minute later, Angie realized it was too logical. This was exactly what Deke would expect her to do. So she had to do something else. No. She thought about it another minute. A plan formed to do the obvious—rent a room as Deke expected her to do, then go somewhere else. But where? She pulled into the least expensive-looking motel and took a Texas map out of her glove compartment. Goliad. The name of the town leaped from the others. It was farther from Rockport than Corpus Christi, but it was closer to the Blackwood ranch. Some instinct told her that Deke would only check Goliad if he found no trace of her in Corpus Christi. But he would find a trace of her here. She was going to make sure of that.

With a new plan, Angie entered the hotel and registered under her own name. After all, she didn't want to make it too difficult for Deke to locate her, and she needed to use her credit card to pay for the week's stay. She couldn't afford to keep draining her supply of cash. She would need that in Goliad.

She carried her suitcase into the room and took out two outfits that she wouldn't be needing. She hung them in the closet. Easily replaceable items like toothpaste, toothbrush, deodorant and hairbrush she left in the bathroom so the room would look occupied. Angie put the rest of her clothes and cosmetics in a disposable laundry bag. Before she left the room, she messed up the bed. Every couple days or so, Angie realized she would have to come back so the management wouldn't become suspicious.

Using a circuitous route, she drove north out of Corpus Christi, then backtracked east to Goliad. Once she found a quiet, out-of-the-way motel, she tied a scarf over her blond hair and put on her sunglasses, then went into the little office. She registered under the name of Patricia Sullivan, borrowing Ted's surname. The motel had monthly rates which were much more economical than paying by the day, so Angie paid for a month in advance, even though it seriously depleted her supply of cash.

By day's end, she was feeling quite proud of herself. The only obstacle left was figuring out a way to see Lindy. There was no telling how long Deke would keep her out of school. It would be foolhardy to try to go to the ranch. Even if Deke wasn't around, he would have left orders barring her from the house. As nerve-wracking as it sounded, the only thing to do was lie low and wait.

It was so much easier said than done. She wanted her presence in Goliad kept quiet, which meant keeping to her motel room as much as possible. It was an escape from boredom to drive to Corpus Christi and maintain her charade there. As the weekend approached, Angie realized that she was getting low on funds. She tried to cash a personal check at a bank in Corpus Christi, but since it was drawn on an out-of-town bank, they politely explained their policy didn't permit it. They did allow her to draw the maximum

73

amount of cash granted by the major credit card she carried, which was enough to get her by until the following week if she was careful.

In the meantime, she waited. By Tuesday of the next week, her patience had run out. Angie drove to the school in Rockport. This time, she didn't venture into the building. Instead, she waited outside in her car and watched for Lindy when the children came out to play during recess. But she didn't see her daughter among them—not that day nor the next.

After school was over on Wednesday, Angie noticed two little girls on their way home coming toward her parked car. They appeared to be Lindy's age. She took a chance that they might be in her class.

"Hello," she called to them, smiling widely to hide her nervousness. "Do either of you know Lindy Blackwood?"

The girls paused a little uncertainly. "Yes," the brown-haired one admitted.

"Was she in school today?" Angie asked.

"No. She's been sick all week."

"And last week, too," the little girl with glasses chimed in.

"Thank you." It confirmed what Angie had already guessed, but it was still bitterly disappointing.

With a heavy heart, she drove back to Goliad. Her evening meal consisted of cheese and crackers and some oranges she'd bought from a man selling fruit out of the back of his pickup along the road. When she counted her money that night, Angie discovered that she had spent more than she realized. She counted again then checked her purse to make certain she had not secreted some bills away. There was none.

For more than an hour, she paced the room trying to decide whether she should drive all the way to Houston tomorrow, hand in her notice at work, close her bank accounts, and inform her landlord she was vacating her apartment. After all, she did intend to move here, but in the end, Angie reached for the telephone.

"Hello, Ted," she said, the minute he answered. "It's me, Angie."

"Angie! How did you know I was just thinking about you?" he laughed with pleasure. Angie didn't realize how lonely she'd been until she heard the warmth and friendship in his voice. "I've missed you," he declared without apology. "I don't know if I can wait until Saturday for you to come back. I'm taking you out to dinner. Where would you like to go?"

"Ted—" She hesitated, trying to find the best way to tell him. But she finally just blurted it out, "I'm not sure I'll be back on Saturday."

"Why?" He shot back. "What's wrong? Where are you?"

"Goliad."

"Wh—" Ted paused. "Should I ask what you're doing there of all places?"

"It's a nice, friendly little town."

"So is Houston. Why don't you come home?" he urged.

"I can't."

"Angie, what's going on? Do you have any idea of how vivid my imagination is?" he demanded. "You're in trouble of some kind. What is it?"

"I'm just low on cash. You don't have a couple hundred you could lend me, do you?" She tried to make a joke out of it.

"Is it money?" Ted was having none of it. "I'll send you some. However much you want."

"Thanks. I might have to take you up on that." But she couldn't bring herself to ask him for it now.

"If you aren't coming back on Saturday, when will you arrive?" He sensed her hesitation. "You have to be to work Monday morning."

Angie took a deep breath. He would know soon enough so she might as well tell him. "I'm quitting, Ted. I've decided to call in my resignation tomorrow."

"You aren't serious," he paused, then concluded, "you are. Why?"

"It's a long story," she murmured lamely.

"I don't know about you, but I've got all night—so why don't you tell it to me?" The compassion, the offer of understanding in his voice was almost too much for Angie. She felt herself choking up.

"Oh, Ted. You don't know what you're saying. You don't want to hear my troubles." She tried to laugh, but it came out as a sob.

"Yes, I do." His gentleness was almost a caress. "Tell me, Angie."

Before she realized what she was doing, she had started pouring out the story of that summer seven years ago, her abortive marriage to Deke, and the baby she'd abandoned to her ex-husband. She told him about the feelings of guilt she'd gone through, the endless wondering whether she'd had a boy or girl, and the haunting knowledge of knowing exactly where her baby was. When she related the moment of meeting with Lindy, Angie cried.

Later, with her emotions under control once more, Angie felt enormously relieved. The terrible tension had gone from her. Confession did seem to be a catharsis for the soul.

"This time I can't walk away from Lindy. That's why I'm not coming back to Houston," she finished, and was amazed to discover she could tease him, "Now, aren't you sorry you asked?"

"No. I only wish that I had asked before," Ted replied in all seriousness. Then he continued in a lighter vein. "I know this may sound prejudiced, but I think what you need is a lawyer, Angie. I happen to know one who might be interested in helping you."

"Oh? And who might that be?" she asked, already guessing.

"Me. Although it isn't exactly my field, I do have a good friend who specializes in custody suits."

"Ted—" She hardly dared to hope. "Do you think there's a chance—"

"I don't know, Angie," he interrupted. "Let me talk to him, sketch in the rough details of your case, and see what his reaction is, okay?"

"Okay," she agreed.

"Is there any way I can get in touch with you?"

"Yes." Angie gave him the name and telephone number of the motel. "I've registered under the name Patricia Sullivan."

"Sullivan?" he repeated with pleased surprise. "I'll take it as a compliment that you borrowed my name."

"I didn't think you'd mind." She smiled at the phone. It was crazy how reassuring it was to know that she had an ally.

"I don't. I'll be talking to you in the next couple of days or so," Ted promised. "Are you going to be all right?"

"I'm fine," Angie assured him. "In fact, I haven't felt this good in a long time. I don't know how I can ever thank you."

"I'll see if I can't come up with a way." And Angie could hear his smile over the phone.

She laughed and wished him good night. There was a peaceful quiet in the room when she hung up the phone. She went straight to bed and had the first, really good night's sleep in nearly two weeks.

The next morning, Angie woke up refreshed and ready to take on the world—maybe even Deke Blackwood. She laughed aloud, glad that she had recovered her sense of humor.

Dressed in blue jeans and her favorite blouse in powder blue silk, Angie treated herself to a big breakfast, then returned to the motel room.

Inaction didn't suit her. She considered driving to Corpus Christi, but she couldn't really afford to use the gasoline. Pausing at the window, she looked outside. It was really a pity that she didn't have an ally like Ted at the Blackwood Ranch so she could secretly arrange to see Lindy. The thought stayed in her mind, germinated and grew. There was a chance—a wild chance—that she had one.

Before she got cold feet, Angie hurried to the phone and put through a call to the Blackwood Ranch. She let it ring and ring, certain there had to be someone at home. Just as she was about to hang up, a woman answered, a little out of breath.

"Marissa?" Angie ventured hesitantly. "Is that you?"

"Yes." The answer came back with a certain inflection of curiosity. "Who's this?"

"I . . . It's Angie." She heard the quick breath taken, followed by silence. "Marissa, please don't hang up. Is Deke there?"

"No. He's out checking cattle this morning," his sister answered cautiously.

"Good," Angie sighed. "I wanted to talk to you." She felt the uncertainty that accompanied Marissa's silence. "How . . . How is Lindy?"

"She's fine." It was a brief reply, noncommunicative.

"I'm glad. At school, they said she was sick and I just wanted to be sure that was . . . a story." It had only been a remote possibility, but Angie was relieved that illness had been given merely as an excuse for Lindy's absence.

"There's nothing.wrong with her, Angie. I promise. She's happy and healthy. Actually, she's enjoying playing hooky." There was a slight pause, then Marissa burst out. "You really took a chance calling here. What if Deke had answered the phone instead of me? You must be crazy to call."

Her heart gave a little lurch of relief because Angie suddenly realized it was going to be all right. Marissa wasn't going to tell Deke she had called. There was some hope after all.

"I am crazy," she admitted. "I'm crazy to be calling, I'm crazy to be here, but I just couldn't stay away any longer. I tried, Marissa. But I just had to see her."

"I guessed it was something like that. Where are you? No." Marissa immediately took back the question. "Don't tell me. I don't want to know. If Deke finds out I've talked to you, he'll worm it out of me. If I don't know, I can't tell him anything."

"I'm sorry. I'm putting you in a terrible position." Angie suddenly realized how selfish she was being. "I shouldn't have called."

"It's okay. I'm a big girl now. I think I can handle my brother," Marissa assured her.

"How's your mother and dad?" Angie inquired, easily visualizing a pair of doting grandparents.

"I . . . guess you don't know. Mom died two years ago from influenza complications and Dad was killed when his light plane crashed on take-off five years ago this month."

"I didn't know." The news left her slightly stunned. "I'm sorry. I . . . remember how excited they were about the baby."

"I know. They worshiped Lindy. Daddy was always going in to wake her up so she'd cry and he'd have an excuse to hold her," Marissa remembered with obvious fondness. "Mom fretted over her constantly, worrying over the least little sniffle or whimper. It was really cute the way Dad used to tease her, insisting that he couldn't believe she was the same woman who had raised Deke and me. It's a miracle they didn't spoil Lindy to distraction."

"How about yourself, Marissa?" Angie was conscious of all that had changed in seven years. There was a tendency to put people and places in limbo, expecting them to be the same and look the same. "What are you doing now? Are you married? Engaged?"

"No, to both." There was a resigned note in her voice. "I was engaged for awhile, but it didn't work out. So, I guess I'll be the spinster sister for awhile and look after my motherless niece." The carelessly spoken remark wasn't meant to be unkind, but Angie couldn't check the involuntary gasp of bitter regret. Realizing what she'd said, Marissa was instantly contrite. "That was a terrible thing to say. Angie, I'm sorry. I didn't mean it the way it sounded."

"I know you didn't. It's all right, really," she assured her, but Angie was painfully aware of the years of separation and all the little things she'd missed—Lindy's first step, her first tooth, her first day of school. It was agony. "What's she like, Marissa?" Tightness gripped her throat. "Tell me about Lindy. There's so much I don't know."

"Oh, Angie," Marissa whispered with touching commiseration. In the pause that followed, Angie had the impression that Marissa was searching for the words to describe her daughter and the little facts that were important in Lindy's eyes. "Right now, her favorite color is lavender, although last summer it was pink. Sometimes she seems as changeable as the wind, but she's just so inquisitive that she can't help trying new things. She's clothes conscious because she wants to look nice, but there's nothing prissy about her. Living on a ranch, Lindy is outside a lot, but she isn't a rough-and-tumble tomboy. She rides. Deke has promised her a horse of her own on her eighth birthday. When she grows up, she wants to be a Dallas Cowboy cheerleader which, in itself, is a blend between glamor and rough sports, I guess."

Angie closed her eyes while her hands tightened their grip on the phone. She was trembling, hurting, silently crying. She didn't dare try to speak for fear her voice would become an incoherent sob. Her throat ached to be released from her determined control of emotion.

"Lindy gets along well with other children her age—makes friends easily," Marissa went on. "She's self-assertive—a leader not a follower. I guess she takes after Deke in that regard. She's extremely bright, but she isn't the know-it-all type. She just likes to learn."

"At school—" There was a rasp in her voice and Angie paused to swallow it before trying again. "—she's in the second grade. She's only six years old."

"Yes. It seems that Mom, Deke, and I taught her too much before she started kindergarten. After the first week she got tired of all that 'baby-stuff' and decided to visit the first grade. It was three days before the teacher realized she had an extra pupil in her class. The school tested her and decided she was capable of doing first grade work, both mentally and psychologically, so she skipped kindergarten and advanced a grade. She hasn't had any trouble at all."

"I wondered," Angie murmured, because there was so much she had wondered about. "Marissa?" She bit her lip, knowing what she was about to ask was wrong. "Is there any chance—I could see her?"

"Oh, Angie." There was a wealth of sympathy, regret and uncertainty in the simple reply.

"Only for a couple of hours. I just want to see her and talk to her for a little bit." Somehow she managed to sound reasonable and not as desperate as she felt.

"Deke would never allow it," his sister protested weakly. "He's become so hard and withdrawn. He's my brother, but we have never really been that close that we talked about personal things. Angie, he won't even discuss the possibility of you having a small part in Lindy's life. I hate to say this, but I don't think he'll ever agree."

That much Angie had already guessed. "Does he have to know?" she suggested. "Couldn't we meet somewhere? You could tell him that you're taking Lindy to the beach or shopping somewhere—a public place."

"Angie, I don't know," Marissa murmured uncertainly.

"Please. I only want to spend a couple hours with her, find out what she's like for myself. I think Deke believes I'll kidnap her. But honestly, I'm not trying to take Lindy away from him," Angie promised.

"Lindy does need a new winter coat for every day. The one she has is too small." The wheels were turning slowly, finding a little traction.

"Then you have a legitimate reason to take her shopping," she affirmed. "I'll meet you somewhere. If Deke should find out, you can say that I followed you there."

"Yes. Yes, that's true. But I do most of my

shopping for Lindy's clothes in Corpus Christi. Deke would never agree to let me take her there because that's where he thinks you are."

"Come to Goliad." She was briefly elated that her sham had worked. Deke didn't suspect she was here.

"Goliad. Is that where . . . ?" Marissa didn't finish the question because she didn't want to know the answer. "Yes, Goliad would be perfect. Have you ever been to the Presidio La Bahia?"

"I know where it is," Angie admitted, even though she hadn't done any sightseeing in the area, staying in the motel room as much as possible.

"We could meet there," Marissa stated.

"When? What time?" Angie couldn't hold back her eagerness.

"I don't want to wait too long or I'll start acting guilty and Deke will suspect something's up," his sister declared, exhaling a heavy breath. "Let's try for tomorrow at one-thirty. If I'm not there, then you'll know that Deke wouldn't agree to letting me take Lindy away from the ranch."

"I understand."

A pickup truck with a horse trailer in tow stopped at the front yard of the main house. The two saddled horses inside the slatted trailer shifted to keep their balance, their iron-shod hooves loud on the reinforced floor.

Deke stepped out of the passenger side of the truck's cab and paused to shoot a steely glance at the driver.

"Pull the left rear shoe on the bay. It's the wrong weight, and it's throwing his stride off." There was a snap in his voice. Deke heard it and knew Ben had done nothing to warrant it.

The response was a somewhat clipped, "Yes, sir."

Sighing a little irritably, Deke swung the cab door shut and stood to one side as the pickup continued on its way to the barns. With heavy strides, he started toward the front entrance of the sprawling ranch house. The single-story structure was built low to the ground with very little slant to its roof. Its thick concrete walls blocked out the summer heat of the subtropical climate and the wide overhang of its roof shaded its windows from the burning rays of the sun.

"Daddy!" Lindy's delighted cry came from his left. The happy sound of her voice lifted the black mood that had been on him. "I thought you wouldn't be back until lunchtime!"

She ran across the grass to intercept him and walk with him to the house, but Deke swept her slight, blue-jeaned figure off the ground and carried her astraddle his hip. He paused to look at her, as if unconsciously needing the reassurance of the sight of her as well as the feel of her.

"Did you miss me?" Deke pretended surprise.

"You know I always miss you, Daddy." She wound her arms around his neck and hugged him.

His arms tightened in a silent response as he buried his face in her tangled blond hair. Just for an instant, its silken texture and fresh scent reminded him of Angie, but Deke crushed the thought from his mind the same way he'd crushed her out of his heart. He lifted his head and glanced sharply around the yard.

"Where's Marissa?" His dark brows arched together, one lifting slightly in question, when he glanced to his daughter.

"She went in the house to answer the phone." Lindy kept a small arm curved around his neck.

When Marissa heard Lindy's cry of greeting, she gripped the phone with both hands in a furtive gesture. "Angie, Deke's coming. I have to hang up. Tomorrow, one-thirty at the Presidio La Bahia."

"I'll be there. Please try to come, if it's at all possible," Angie pleaded.

"I will." Behind her, she could hear the turning of the front door knob and wanted to hang up quickly before Deke discovered she was on the phone. Marissa instantly realized if he saw her hanging up so hurriedly, he'd probably get suspicious. In the space of the same thought, she came up with an idea, but there wasn't time to warn Angie of her intention. The door was opening. In a voice loud enough for him to hear, she said brightly, "I'll ask Deke and see what he says, then call you back this afternoon. Okay?"

"What?" Angie's voice was startled. "You aren't going to tell him?"

"No, I won't, silly," Marissa laughed, acutely aware of the footsteps approaching the living room.

There was the slightest pause, then Angie guessed, "Deke is there. He can hear you."

"Yes, that's right," Marissa affirmed in the same light and false tone. "'Bye. I'll talk to you later." Lindy bounded into view as she heard Angie echo her words and the line go dead. Marissa half-turned, the telephone receiver still to her ear, and pretended that she had just became aware of her brother's presence in the house. His hard gaze was sharply questioning, as she had known it would be.

"Wait a minute," she said quickly into the phone. "Deke just walked in. Let me ask—" She faked a pause. "Hello?" With a sigh, she turned to hang up the phone, but her heart was beating a mile a minute. She felt guilty at the way she was deliberately deceiving her brother.

"Who was on the phone?" Deke queried.

Marissa was ready with her lie, support for it had already been provided by another phone call earlier in the morning. "Cindy Coulson. She and Don are having a barbeque a week from Sunday and she called to invite us." All of it was true except the part that she had just this minute been talking to Cindy. "I said I'd mention it to you and let her know." She finally faced him and was relieved to see he'd already lost interest in the phone call.

He swept off his hat, running a hand through his dark hair. "You might as well let her know we won't be attending."

"I'll call her later." Marissa tried hard to sound offhand and turned her attention to Lindy. "I suppose you two are ready for lunch."

"I'm starved," Lindy insisted.

"You always are," Marissa smiled and lifted her gaze to Deke. "How about you?"

"I can wait," he replied indifferently. "No rush."

For a brief instant, Marissa honestly wondered if her brother ever had needs like hunger, thirst and sleep, which of course he did. There was even a woman in Corpus Christi who relieved his sexual urges. He probably thought she didn't know about that but she did. It was just that he was so hard and unfeeling. Deke had never talked about what had gone wrong with his forced marriage to Angie. After Lindy was born, he'd come back to Texas with her. Marissa had never believed him when he had declared Angie didn't want the baby. The phone call today from Angie proved she had been right.

Forcing a smile, she crouched down to her niece. "Let's get your jacket off." It stretched tightly across the shoulders, the seams threatening to burst their threads. "You're growing like a weed, Lindy. We're going to have to buy you a new jacket."

"This one is too small," Lindy agreed.

"How would you like to go shopping in Corpus Christi tomorrow and we'll buy a new one?" Marissa suggested brightly and watched the girl's face light up.

"No!" The explosive denial from Deke nearly made Marissa jump out of her skin, even though she'd been expecting it. Even Lindy looked startled by his barely suppressed anger and turned a half-frightened look at him. It was Lindy who prompted him to temper the harshness from his voice. "You aren't going shopping tomorrow."

"Why not?" Lindy wanted to know.

"Because I said you're not." Deke came back with a hard-bitten answer that refused to discuss it.

"Go wash your hands for lunch," Marissa instructed, rather than argue with Deke in front of his child. She waited until Lindy was out of the room before she straightened to confront her brother. "You are being totally unreasonable."

"She can get by without a new jacket for awhile longer," Deke stated. "It isn't something that has to be purchased tomorrow or even next week."

"No, it isn't," Marissa agreed. "But she needs to get out. Lindy has been cooped up here for almost two weeks. How much longer are you going to keep her a prisoner in her own home?"

"That's my affair!" he snapped. "It doesn't concern you."

"It concerns Lindy, so therefore, it concerns me!" she retorted just as sharply. "What is the harm in taking Lindy to Corpus Christi to shop for a new coat?"

"You know damn well Angie's there!" he hurled at her savagely, the first break in his control that she'd seen.

"So what?" Marissa argued. "I'll be with Lindy. You can't keep her locked up forever."

"No."

"All right, I won't take her to Corpus Christi," she pretended to concede. "We'll do our shopping in Goliad. But Lindy needs to get out—at least for a few hours." She held her breath, noting his hesitation. "You know I'm right, Deke."

"Okay." He gave in with grim reluctance. "Take her to Goliad, but you be back here by four o'clock."

"I will," Marissa promised, and felt guilty for deceiving him when he so obviously trusted her.

Chapter Five

$\mathcal{T}$ he massive stone walls marked the perimeters of the Presidio Santa Maria del Loreto de la Bahia, established in 1749. This Spanish fort, or *presidio*, was built to protect the Mission Espiritu Santo a mile to the north.

Under the serenity of a Texas blue sky, its barracks, chapel and the other structures enclosed within its protective walls stood quietly. There was nothing about its silent grounds to reveal its infamous place in Texas history. Nothing to tell that once the companion cry to "Remember the Alamo!" had been "Remember Goliad!"

On March 6, 1836, the Alamo fell after thirteen days of glory holding off the siege of the Mexican Army under the command of Generalissimo Santa Anna. One hundred and eighty-seven "Texians" died at the Alamo—the expected help from Colonel James W. Fannin, Jr. and his men never came. Fannin was at Goliad, where his scouts brought back reports that led him to believe the main force of the Mexican Army would come his way. So he maintained his position at Goliad to defend it.

But when the Mexican Army massed against him at the end of March, Fannin had the choice of fighting till the death of the last man, as those at the Alamo had done, or surrender. He elected not to sacrifice the lives of the 342 men in his command and accepted Santa Anna's terms of surrender. Fannin and his men were imprisoned within the walls of the Presidio La Bahia along the banks of the same San Antonio River that flowed past the Alamo. On the last Sunday in March, Palm Sunday, Santa Anna violated the terms of surrender and ordered the massacre of Colonel Fannin and all 342 Texans.

"Remember Goliad!" became a rallying cry for the Texas Revolution, a poignant phrase that was echoed after the glory of "Remember the Alamo!" A few hundred yards outside the wall of the *presidio,* a monument marks the grave of Fannin and his men.

It was inside the walls by the chapel where Angie waited. She glanced anxiously at her watch. It showed thirty-six minutes past the hour of one. Something must have gone wrong. Just as she looked up, she saw a tall, dark-haired woman walk around the corner of the building—a blond-haired child skipping at her side. Although she'd only seen her once before, Angie recognized her daughter, Lindy, immediately and experienced a rush of elation.

Hurrying forward to meet them, she could hardly take her eyes off Lindy. When she finally looked at Marissa, her smile was warm with gratitude. Her friend of seven years ago had matured into a handsome woman with clean, strong features.

"It's good to see you again, Marissa," Angie said, and meant it.

"I had forgotten how beautiful you are. No wonder I was so popular that summer until—" She stopped, not finishing the sentence, but Angie guessed that Marissa meant until Deke met her and monopolized her free time.

"Thank you." Angie accepted the compliment without any reference to what had been left unsaid and looked down at the little girl. Her blue eyes darkened with love. "Hello, Lindy."

"I remember you. You visited school one day," Lindy said in recognition.

"Yes, the day you found the rock with the fossil in it." A stiff breeze whipped her hair, swirling amber strands across her face. She tucked them behind her ear. "I wondered if you'd remember me," Angie admitted.

"Your name's Angie," Lindy recalled.

"That's right," she smiled, but inside she was scared. She wanted so much for Lindy to like her, but she suddenly didn't know what to say to her. She wanted to take Lindy in her arms and just hold her—but she couldn't, of course. So she ran a caressing hand across the front of Lindy's plum-colored jacket. "That's a pretty coat you're wearing."

"It's new. Marissa bought it for me today," Lindy informed her.

Angie had thought as much since the warm day didn't require a jacket that heavy. "I like it."

"Thank you. So do I. It's my favorite color." Her interest switched to a different topic. "Have you been here before? Do you know what's over there?" She pointed to the far corner of the walled enclosure."

"No. This is my first visit to the *presidio*," Angie admitted.

Lindy turned to look up at her aunt. "Can we go over there and see?"

Marissa glanced at Angie to be sure she had no objections to her precious time with Lindy being used in this manner. Since she was able to go with her daughter and share her experience in a new place, Angie didn't mind.

"Sure. Let's go look," Marissa agreed with the request to explore. For Lindy's benefit, she went through the motions of officially including Angie. "You'll come, too, won't you, Angie?"

"Yes," she accepted at once and fell in step with them, Lindy walking in the middle.

It soon became apparent that Lindy was too impatient to walk. She'd dart ahead, a miniature dynamo of energy, then wait with a great show of forbearance for Angie and Marissa to catch up with her.

Finally Marissa suggested, "Why don't you run ahead, Lindy, and we'll follow?" But Lindy didn't jump at the idea. Instead she hung back. "What's the matter? I thought you were in a hurry to see what was over there."

"I promised Daddy I'd stay close to you," Lindy explained.

"He just didn't want us to get separated. I'll still be able to see you if you run ahead," Marissa assured her, and she didn't need to explain to Angie why Deke had extracted the promise from his daughter. Angie watched Lindy tear off across the parade grounds to the far wall. For several yards, she and Marissa walked together with neither breaking the silence until Marissa finally spoke. "I wish we'd kept in touch. I never did understand why you ran away to Arizona."

"I was seventeen, confused and scared— and pregnant." She lifted her shoulders in an expressive little shrug. "Everyone was deciding what was best for me and nobody was asking how I felt. They were pushing me into a marriage that I wasn't sure I wanted. So I ran off to my uncle's in Arizona, but they all followed me—my aunt, Deke, your parents."

"I thought you wanted to marry Deke." Marissa looked at her with some surprise. "You were in love with him, weren't you?"

"I thought I was in love with him during the summer, then when I found out I was pregnant, it all suddenly became different. He seemed like a stranger." There was a confused shake of her head, unable to sort it out even now. "It's hard to explain."

"But, after you were married, surely—" Marissa began, but Angie interrupted her.

"We never lived together as man and wife." She went on to explain, "The day we were married I asked him whether he'd have married me if I hadn't been pregnant and Deke admitted that he probably wouldn't have. I was only seventeen, but I knew a baby wasn't a good enough reason for two people to marry. Of course, Deke said we could make it work. How could it when we were both being forced into it?"

"I can't believe that Deke felt that way." It was difficult for Marissa to accept that anyone could force her brother into doing something he didn't want.

"He did. He didn't even treat me the same way he used to," Angie remembered. Before Deke hadn't been able to keep his hands off her, and afterward he'd been reluctant to touch her. "So I stayed at my uncle's. It gave me a lot of time to think."

"About Lindy," Marissa guessed. Deke's claim that Angie hadn't wanted Lindy had always bothered her. "Did you give her up willingly?"

"Willingly?" she repeated the adverb on a painfully amused note. "I don't think any mother gives up her child *willingly*. I had time to do a lot of thinking. I'd like to believe that I did what was best for her. I had nothing to give her but my love. Deke could give her that, plus a home and all the other advantages of money and position."

"I think I understand now," his sister murmured and paused, reaching out to warmly clasp Angie's hand.

"That means a lot to me," Angie replied, discovering again that she had found a friend.

Lindy came racing back, out of breath. "It's just a wall. I looked, but I can't find any way to get up on top," she panted.

"That's just as well," Marissa laughed. "You'd probably fall and break a leg."

"Where shall we go now?" Lindy wanted to know.

"Let's look through the museum," Angie suggested.

"Okay," Lindy agreed with alacrity.

This time Lindy was content to walk with them as they recrossed the yard to the stone structure in the *presidio* that housed the museum. Angie fielded most of her daughter's non-stop chatter, while Marissa deliberately played a minor role in the conversartion.

In the museum, Marissa lagged behind the mother and daughter pair, giving them a chance to get acquainted. Lindy was quick to take advantage of the tolerance of her companion to ask endless questions about the artifacts on display, exposing the curiosity Angie had only been told about before.

As they left the museum and walked out into the bright Texas sunshine, Lindy unselfconsciously slipped her hand into Angie's. Her heart swelled with a radiant joy at the innocent gesture of trust. In her happiness, Angie forgot all the pain of the past. Marissa was somewhere behind them, she knew, but for the moment this little part of the world contained only herself and Lindy.

Slowing her steps, Lindy looked up at Angie and tipped her head at an inquiring angle. "Haven't you got tired of answering all my questions?"

"I haven't yet," Angie smiled.

"You're nice," Lindy concluded as if it had been in question.

"Thank you." Angie was deeply moved by the unsolicited compliment and tried not to show how much it affected her. "I like you, too. I know any mother would be proud to have a little girl like you."

"I don't have a mother. She died when I was born," Lindy declared in an off-hand way and started walking again.

"Do you . . . Do you ever wonder what she was like?" Her casual inquiry faltered.

"Yes," Lindy nodded, not at all upset by the question. "I asked Daddy about her once."

"Oh?" Angie hesitated, aware of Deke's opinion of her. "What did he tell you?"

"He told me she was the most beautiful girl in the whole world," Lindy skipped along beside her for a few paces, then resumed a walk, looking off into the distance as if reliving the conversation. "He said I was going to look just like her when I grew up. She had blond hair, too, like me. Only her eyes were blue—a midnight blue, he said, like a Texas sky full of stars." With a sideways glance at Angie she declared, "He loved her more than anything."

Angie was grateful that Deke had given Lindy a beautiful memory of her mother, except that she knew he hadn't done it as a kindness to her. He had done it solely for Lindy's sake.

"I'm sure your daddy loves you, too," she murmured.

"Oh, he does," Lindy replied without hesitation. "But when he loved my mother, I wasn't born yet."

"I had forgotten that," Angie admitted, silently marveling that her daughter was able to make the distinction.

A little frown appeared on the child's forehead. "I think Daddy still misses her. That's why he doesn't smile very much." She paused and turned to Angie, an earnest expression sweeping over her face. "One time I was sick and Daddy stayed with me. When I woke up, he had tears in his eyes. He said it was because he was afraid he might lose me and he was happy I was better."

"I'll bet he was very happy," Angie agreed huskily.

"I'm never going to leave my daddy," Lindy stated.

"No, you're never going to leave your daddy," Angie barely whispered the words.

"Angie, Lindy," Marissa called to them, and the pair turned as she approached. Regret was in the glance she directed to Angie. "It's after three." Then she reminded Lindy, "We promised your dad we'd be home by four."

"I remember." Lindy released Angie's hand to stand with her aunt. "I want to show him my new coat."

Marissa smiled apologetically, regretting that she had to be the one to bring Angie's afternoon with her daughter to an end. "I'm sorry."

Tears stung the back of her eyes as Angie shook her head in a definite dismissal of the apology. "No matter what happens, I'll always be grateful for what you've done. Thank you." She quickly hugged her friend. With overly bright eyes, Angie crouched down to Lindy. Not knowing when she might see her daughter again, she wanted to make the most of the moment, and she ached with a love that she couldn't show. "How about a hug, Lindy?" Her voice wavered on the light note.

Lindy's hesitation was slight. Naturally affectionate, she curved her arms around Angie's neck to embrace her. A knee touched the ground for balance as Angie held her daughter closer, closing her eyes tightly to shut off the sudden rush of tears.

"You take care of yourself and be good," Angie whispered and drew back to smooth the white-gold hair away from Lindy's cheek.

"I will," Lindy nodded, not quite under-standing the strong undercurrents of emotion she sensed.

"Angie." Marissa's suddenly anxious tone triggered an alarm.

The instant Angie glanced up, she saw the reason. Deke was standing at the exit, poised in a motionless stance like a predator before it moves in for the kill. Her heart was pounding in her throat as adrenaline rushed through her system, heightening all her senses.

"Daddy!" Lindy finally saw the object of their attention and abandoned Angie to race to his side.

Angie slowly straightened to stand erect, riveted by his steel gaze. Deke paid scant attention to Lindy and her excited chattering, except to place a possessive hand on her shoulder and press her to the length of his leg.

"Angie—" Marissa murmured.

"Remember—you didn't know I was here," Angie reminded her, without glancing away from Deke. She didn't want Deke directing his anger at Marissa.

Scarcely thirty feet separated them, yet it seemed to take forever to cross it. Her nerve ends quivered under the rake of his eyes. It was all she could do to keep from bolting and running away. The teak-hard contours of his features were too blatantly virile, his looks too strikingly dominant. Power was etched in every muscled limb of his body.

Not until Angie reached him did his gaze flick to his sister. "Take Lindy to the car."

"Deke—" Marissa attempted a protest.

But he cut across it with a threateningly quiet, "Now." He firmly pushed Lindy toward her aunt.

"Aren't you coming with us, Daddy?" Lindy was suddenly worried, aware something was wrong.

"No. I'll follow you home. Go with your aunt," Deke ordered. Even when he wasn't looking directly at her, Angie knew he was aware of every breath she drew. She held her silence, like Deke, wanting Lindy to be out of hearing before it all erupted.

Lindy tried to twist her hand out of Marissa's grasp. "I want to ride with you, Daddy."

"Do as you're told." His harsh retort froze the child. Lindy didn't know what she had done to make him so angry. The confusion was in her face as she let Marissa lead her away.

"You shouldn't take it out on Lindy just because you're angry with me," Angie told him and felt the full censure of his gaze.

"I have no intention of taking it out on anyone but you," Deke assured her with menacing calm.

Angie would rather have faced the fury of his temper than this icy control. Her first priority, above her own defense, was to protect Marissa. She owed his sister that much—and more.

"Before you say anything, Deke, I know what you're probably thinking," she began, "but Marissa didn't know I was here. I followed her—"

"Liar." His low voice slashed her with contempt.

Angie hesitated and tried again. "I swear she had no part in this."

"Do you really think I'd believe anything you say?" Deke taunted.

"But—"

"You persuaded my own sister to betray me," he accused, and when Angie would have denied it, he didn't give her a chance to speak. "Don't try to convince me that you followed her here, because you won't succeed. One of my men followed Marissa and Lindy today." His statement splintered through her and his gaze narrowed on her startled expression with grim complacency. "You didn't anticipate that, did you?"

"No," Angie admitted numbly.

"You were already here waiting for Marissa when she arrived. My man spotted your car in the parking lot and checked the license plates."

"Then he called you," she realized.

"Yes."

"I only wanted to see Lindy—talk to her," Angie tried to explain. "No harm was done."

His gaze swept her with freezing disgust. "No harm was done, is that right? You only persuaded my sister to meet you behind my back. I suppose Lindy has been told to keep this afternoon a secret from me—her own father!" On that blistering note, Angie started to avert her head, but Deke imprisoned her chin between his fingers, his grip hard and punishing. "My own blood! And you were arranging for them to lie to me! But no harm's been done!"

His bruising hold forced her head back. She couldn't even get her mouth open to answer. Her fingers circled his sinewed wrist in mute protest. Angie could feel the violence deep within him and saw it in the tight curl of his lips. Deke abruptly released her and she began trembling in a delayed reaction to the brush with danger.

"It isn't going to do any good to threaten me, Deke." Angie wouldn't back down, regardless of his physical intimidation. "You're not going to keep me away from Lindy."

For a long second, he merely looked at her. "Where are you staying?" When she hesitated, his mouth thinned. "Don't bother to tell me Corpus Christi, because I already know better."

She didn't bother to ask him how. "Here, in Goliad." She gave him the name of the motel, knowing he'd find it sooner or later.

"I'll meet you there at seven this evening," Deke stated.

"You'll meet me?" Angie couldn't believe she'd heard him correctly.

"Yes." There was a deliberate pause. "That is, if you want to discuss your chances of seeing Lindy."

"I do," she assured him with a rush. "Tonight, at seven." Angie was dazed by his unexpected capitulation to talk to her about Lindy. It was a complete turnabout, totally out of character.

"Good." There was a glint in his eyes that she didn't like as he turned and walked away. Deke seemed altogether too pleased.

It made her uneasy, but Angie couldn't throw away the chance that he was serious. It was possible that she'd managed to convince him she wasn't going to give up. Maybe he was willing to negotiate some kind of agreement that would allow her visiting privileges.

Angie was still trying to puzzle out his motives when she reached the parking lot. By that time, there was no sign of Deke and she was no closer to an answer than she'd been before.

Chapter Six

At five o'clock, Angie was back in her motel room. It was two hours before she had to meet Deke and she was still regarding it with a great deal of uncertainty. She went through the meager wardrobe she had along, trying to choose an outfit that would be casual yet give her some much-needed confidence. After much indecision, she laid out taupe slacks and a matching blazer jacket and draped a silk blouse of brown and gold paisley print on the chair. With that accomplished, Angie entered the bathroom to shower before changing.

She was in the midst of toweling dry when she heard the knock on her door. Her wristwatch was on the sink counter. It wasn't even six o'clock yet. It couldn't be Deke. Angie frowned and shrugged into her terrycloth beachrobe that doubled for a dressing gown, although it only reached to mid-thigh. She quickly tied a knot in the cloth belt around her waist.

As she crossed to the door, there was a second knock. She paused not opening it. A sense of caution made her ask, "Who is it?"

"Angie? It's me, Ted." The intervening walls and door partially muffled his voice but she still recognized it.

"Ted." Angie opened the door to stare at him in disbelief, surprise halting her smile in mid-curve.

The jacket of his dark business suit was draped behind one shoulder, suspended by the hook of one finger. His other hand rested against the door frame, giving the impression that it was propping him up. The striped tie was unknotted and hanging loose down his front, the top buttons of his white shirt unfastened. A lazy smile softened his square-jawed face.

"If the moutain won't come to Mohammed—" he said and left the rest unfinished.

"I can't believe it! What are you doing here?" Angie automatically opened the door to admit him as Ted reached down to pick up his briefcase and a small weekender bag sitting outside the door. "Why didn't you let me know you were coming?"

"I wanted to surprise you." He walked into her room and Angie gave the door a push to shut it, not bothering to see if it latched and locked automatically.

"Surprise isn't the word for it," she insisted.

"And here I thought you were wearing that fetching little outfit just for me," Ted grinned with an appreciative glance at the brevity of the robe and its plunging neckline.

"I just got out of the shower." But she made sure the front of her robe snuggly overlapped.

"Then it's a pity I didn't arrive five minutes sooner," he teased.

"I wouldn't have let you in," Angie retorted, then realized, "you still haven't told me what you're doing here?"

"It's a combination of business and pleasure—with emphasis on the pleasure." He tossed his jacket on the bed and caught hold of her shoulders. "I was sitting in Houston with the whole weekend ahead of me and my favorite girl out of town. All of a sudden it came to me—why should both of us be lonely when we can be together? And here I am. Are you glad to see me?"

"Of course." But Angie knew very well it was the promise of companionship that interested her, even if Ted had less platonic intentions.

When he tilted his head toward hers, she lifted her mouth to his kiss. Its pressure was firm, seeking more of a response than she gave. Before it became demanding, Angie eluded it, pushing away with a smile to soften her rejection of his advances. For once, Ted didn't protest.

"I can be patient awhile longer," he smiled, a possessive light darkening his hazel eyes. "Now that you've told me about your child, I know you can be swept away by desire."

"Don't . . . be too sure," Angie murmured, because she knew the truth had become almost the exact opposite.

Ted eyed her for a curious second, then changed the direction of their conversation. "Speaking of your little girl, how are things going here?"

"Maybe not too bad. I saw her today," she told him, unaware of the radiance that entered her expression. "Marissa—that's Deke's sister—brought Lindy to the *presidio*. We spent the afternoon together."

"Did you have permission to do that from your ex-husband?" Ted frowned. "I thought he had forbidden you to see her."

"He had," she admitted.

"But his sister brought her anyway? That sounds like she's on your side," he concluded.

"I think so, but I doubt if it will help." Angie sighed and chewed at the inside of her lower lip. "Deke found out. I'm meeting him tonight at seven to talk about Lindy. That's why I said maybe things aren't so bad."

"But you're not sure?" Ted eyed her curiously.

"With Deke? No, I'm never sure," she answered quite forcefully. Deke was very much an unknown quantity.

"Is he still in love with you?"

"Deke? He despises me." Angie knew that much for certain.

"Since you're meeting him tonight, I think it's a good thing I'm here," Ted stated. "It's sensible to have your legal counsel present during any discussions of this nature."

"You're right." She'd be glad for his support, although she guessed that Deke wouldn't welcome Ted's presence. "Did you have a chance to talk to your friend—the attorney who specializes in custody cases?"

"Yes. That was the business purpose of my trip here," Ted smiled. "And it makes it deductible."

"What did he say?" That's what Angie wanted to know.

"Sam was reluctant to venture an opinion until he'd had a chance to examine the legal documents relating to your divorce and custody of the child. You do have copies, don't you?"

"Yes, but—not with me. They're in a safety deposit box at the bank along with my birth certificate and some other papers," Angie explained.

"In Houston?"

"Yes," she nodded.

"I thought that would be the case." Ted picked up his briefcase and set it on the bed, snapping the latches to open it. "I brought a power of attorney form for you to sign, giving me the right to remove the papers from the safety deposit box. That will save you a trip to Houston."

Ted sat on the edge of the bed and went through the business folders in the case until he found the one containing the document. Taking it out, he closed the lid of the briefcase and laid the paper on it. He offered Angie the ballpoint pen from his shirt pocket.

Using his briefcase for a hard surface to write on, Angie perched on the edge of the bed and signed her name in the signature blank, then returned the pen to Ted. He put the pen into his pocket and replaced the document in his briefcase.

"Is your little girl as beautiful as you are?" he asked.

"I'm too prejudiced," Angie laughed and stayed seated on the bed, facing Ted. "She does have blond hair, but her eyes are gray." Suddenly she was very serious. "Do I have a chance of obtaining visiting rights?"

"There is always a chance, but we simply aren't going to know how good it is until we have studied the final decrees," Ted explained without raising false hopes. "We'll pursue every possibility, Angie. I promise you that."

"Since my parents died, I've never had anyone who really cared about me—no one I could turn to when I was in trouble who was willing to help. I was always a burden—an inconvenience to my relatives—somebody else's problem that had been dumped in their lap—until now." She laid her hand against his smoothly shaven cheek in a warm caress. His presence proved his offer of help hadn't been an idle one, spoken and forgotten. "I've always liked you, Ted. Now I know why."

He covered her hand with his, holding it and turning his head to kiss the inner palm. His hazel eyes were bright and possessive in their study of her face.

"I've needed you almost from the moment we met, Angie. I've been waiting a long time for you to need me," he declared huskily. "You never seemed vulnerable. You were always so independent, self-contained, and in control of yourself and your life."

"It might have seemed that way." Angie didn't try to withdraw her hand, letting him hold it against his face.

But Ted wasn't content with that innocent caress and reached out, placing a hand at the back of her waist to pull her to him. Angie didn't resist his firmly gentle invitation to embrace on the edge of the bed. As they leaned toward each other, Ted paused, his face mere inches from hers.

"I never guessed that you were a woman with a past," he murmured and closed the space between them.

The ardency of his kiss was a pleasant experience. Angie enjoyed it, but the feeling of detachment remained. It didn't move her as it did him. Her arms circled him, trained to respond as her lips were, but the fires inside her remained banked, no force invading to flame them out of control.

So her mind went on thinking calmly while

his mouth hungrily tasted her lips. A woman with a past—she had never thought of herself in those terms. She had kept her secret because "divorced with a child" would have been a red flag waved at every single man she met—and some who weren't single. Her looks alone had drawn sufficent advances—advances that wouldn't have been so easily or quickly turned aside if they had known about her past.

When Ted released her mouth, his lips sought the curve of her neck. His moist nibbles sent tiny shivers over her skin, but none that rocked her. Angie curled a hand into the fine hair at the back of his head, tipping her own head to one side and allowing him freer access to her sensitive throat. His roaming hands arched her closer until she appeared to be straining toward him. Her eyes were half-closed in absent introspection.

A single knock at the door opened them. Her eyes widened as the door swung open from the impetus of that single knock. It hadn't latched when she'd pushed it shut! A cold wave raced through her when Angie saw Deke framed in the doorway. His gray eyes blazed at the sight of her on the bed, locked in a seemingly passionate embrace with a strange man. With his back to the door, Ted was aroused to the state where he was aware of nothing but the woman in his arms.

Recovering from the initial shock, Angie tried to push away from Ted but his arms tightened to hold her there. "It's Deke," she protested frantically, conscious that he was crossing the threshold.

Something of her panic must have communicated itself to Ted, because he relaxed his hold and sent a dazed glance over his shoulder. By then, Deke was striding toward the bed, a wild fury raging in his look. It sobered Ted in an instant, even as it deprived Angie of her voice. Ted let her go and started to rise to confront the man who had invaded their privacy—not instantly making the connection that this was her ex-husband.

"Hey! What do you—" Ted never had an opportunity to finish his challenge as Deke buried a fist in his stomach, doubling him over.

All of it was happening too fast for Angie to react. As Ted bent over, the breath driven out of him, Deke grabbed him by the shoulders and heaved him into the corner. Only the chair with her clothes on it prevented Ted from being shoved head-first into the wall. He crashed into it and fell sideways against the wall.

With a whispered outcry of concern, Angie darted from the bed to go to Ted's aid. But Deke was in her way and she realized that he intended to finish the beating he started. She hurled herself at Deke, throwing her arms around him. Ted was already half-senseless, unable to defend himself.

"Stop it, Deke!" she screamed her panic,

clutching at him when he tried to push her away. "You'll kill him!"

For a split second, Angie thought she was going to be tossed aside. His hands had already taken much of her weight, then the violence of his gaze locked with the terror of hers. She sensed the power struggle within Deke, warring to bring his rage under control. Watching him withdraw into himself and harden was nearly as awesome as his fury. It had passed and Angie sagged weakly in his hold, briefly relieved.

Behind her, there was movement. She twisted her head to look over her shoulder as Ted groped to stand up, shaking his head in an effort to clear it. Except for being dazed, he appeared unharmed. Deke's hold on her relaxed, her flesh tingling where his hands had gripped her so brutally, but she wasn't released. Ted lifted his head to glare at Deke. Outrage darkened Ted's expression.

"I'll have you arrested for assault," Ted charged. "Angie, call the police."

"No," she whispered, but neither man took any notice of her protest.

Deke released her and swung away, his long stride carrying him to the telephone by the bed. Angie thought he was going to rip it out of the wall. He picked it up, volatile anger simmering beneath every move, and thrust the receiver toward Ted.

"Go ahead and call the police," Deke challenged with cold disdain for the threat. "It will be my word against yours. I don't know who the hell you are, mister, but you're in *my* territory. And my word carries a helluva lot more weight than yours!"

Angie was caught literally and figuratively in the middle, not knowing which way to turn. She divided her glances between the two men, but Ted was the logical one to listen to reason. She directed her first appeal to him.

"Ted, this is Lindy's father. Deke Blackwood." After she had identified him by name and saw Ted draw back in reappraisal of the situation, Angie turned to Deke. "Ted Sullivan is a friend of mine from Houston."

"I did have the impression you knew him." There was a faint ring of sarcasm in Deke's reply as he pivoted to roughly shove the telephone back on its place on the bed's night table.

"I also happen to be Angie's attorney," Ted snapped.

Deke's gaze ran sharply between the two of them, harsh and condemning. "I suppose you were 'conferring' with your client when I came to the door," he taunted. "I'm surprised you didn't make a mockery of all this by referring to Angie as 'Miss Hall,' considering the 'intimate conference' I interrupted. Your 'seduction strategy' will have to be postponed." Deke reached, grabbing Ted's suit jacket from the bed and throwing it at him.

Angie paled, realizing how damning it looked—Ted with his jacket and his shirt half-unbuttoned and herself naked under the short robe. Even more damning was Ted's suitcase sitting on the floor by her bed.

"Get your coat on and get out!" Deke ordered.

"He just arrived a few minutes ago," Angie tried to explain.

"You don't have any right to order me out of this room!" Ted defied him. His hands were throttling the jacket Deke had thrown at him as though Ted wished it was Deke's throat.

Deke pinned Angie with a hard look. "You may recall we were to meet tonight to discuss *my* daughter." He sarcastically reminded her of their planned meeting and stressed his custody of their child.

Before she could respond, Ted spoke up, "And *I* will be acting as Angie's counsel during that meeting."

Deke's jaw hardened with displeasure and thinning patience. Outside of a brief glance flicked in Ted's direction, he didn't release Angie from his stabbing look.

"You have a choice of talking to him or me tonight," Deke stated bluntly. "I suggest you order him out if you cherish any hope that I'll give you permission to see Lindy." And he knew very well he wasn't giving her any choice.

"Don't let him blackmail you, Angie," Ted forestalled her answer. "A court of law will decide when you may see your daughter."

Deke slowly turned to study Ted. The corners of his mouth lifted in a half-smile that was arrogantly complacent. Angie looked at him with a definite feeling of unease. He was altogether too sure of himself.

"Have you read the document Angie signed giving the child to me?" Deke asked the question as if he already knew Ted hadn't.

Ted faltered under the steady gaze of the man who appeared so certain of his superior position, then darted a quick glance at Angie, but he didn't admit he hadn't seen the official papers yet. "I haven't had an opportunity to study them thoroughly. That was among the reasons for my trip here from Houston."

"Well, when you do go over them," Deke said smoothly, "I believe you'll find that it won't be up to the law to decide whether Angie ever sees Lindy. I will."

Angie felt her chances slipping away and fixed her gaze on Ted. She wasn't reassured by the doubt and lack of confidence in his expression. But he still attempted to support her claim.

"Regardless of the validity of a given document, the circumstances leading up to it have to be taken into consideration," Ted bluffed. "At the time, Angie was a minor—"

"She had the benefit of legal advice," Deke interrupted. "So did her guardian. Angie knew precisely what she was signing."

Ted looked at her in silent question. "It's true. I did," she admitted, and knew by his reaction that her hopes had been dashed to the ground.

The grounds for any further discussion were

eliminated. Deke stressed the point by picking up Ted's suitcase and hauling his briefcase off the bed, then walked to the open door and tossed them outside.

"Miss Hall won't be needing your services, Mr. Sullivan," Deke stated in cool dismissal. "So your presence here is no longer required or wanted."

Stubbornly, Ted hesitated and moved to stand in front of Angie. "If you don't want me to go, just say so. It'll take an army to get me out of here." He flashed a look of dislike at Deke. "I don't like the idea of you being alone with him."

But Deke had already issued his ultimatum and Angie had known what her choice would have to be. "I'll be all right," she assured Ted. "You'd better go."

His mouth was compressed into a grim line as he turned from her and walked to the door Deke held open. Ted paused to issue his parting threat. "If you lay a hand on her, I'll—"

Deke interrupted, "You may not mind taking another man's leavings, but I'm more particular." Then Deke let an expression of forbidding anger darken his features. "Now, get out!"

Before Ted had crossed the threshold, Deke was already swinging the door shut with a vehemence that had Angie cringing inwardly. But there was no sign of it when he turned to face her, only a slight flaring of his nostrils to attest to its previous existence. Angie felt the run of her nerves as she faced him, all raw masculinity, male features carved in austerely handsome lines and a leanly muscled physique stamped with prepotency. Angie quivered, growing hot under his silvery look. This was the man who had fathered her child and she was alone with him. Her glance swung to the bed, too conscious of its presence in the room.

Chapter Seven

$\mathcal{D}$id you really believe that lover boy was going to be able to help you take Lindy away from me?" Deke's voice was heavy with scorn.

"Ted is a friend," Angie insisted, reacting to his first accusation. "Regardless of how it might have looked, he isn't—and never has been my lover."

An eyebrow was lifted in mocking reproof. "I suppose his suitcase just 'happened' to be sitting by your bed. He never had any intention of spending the weekend in this room— with you."

"He might have 'hoped' it would work out like that," Angie retorted, because she suspected it was what Ted had in mind. "I wasn't expecting him, so I really couldn't say. When he arrived here, I was surprised and invited him in without paying any attention to where he put his suitcase!"

In the ensuing silence, Angie became aware that Deke's attention had shifted to the front of her robe. Something smouldered in his look. She glanced down, discovering the over-lapping fold of her robe had loosened to expose the full swell of her breasts. Flushing, she pulled it more tightly across her front and checked the knotted sash securing it.

Averting her face from his too astute eyes, Angie walked over to set up the chair Ted had tipped over and pick up her clothes from the floor. "My relationship with Ted isn't any of your business." She didn't want to discuss that topic with Deke—and it's implication of sex. "And as for Lindy—I'm not trying to take her away from you. Her home is with you. I only want to be able to visit her."

"That's what you say now." Deke made it plain that he didn't believe her. "Seven years ago this next March, you didn't even want to see the infant you had given birth to. You swore you never would want to see her."

"I was wrong," she admitted in irritation.

"You're claiming now that you only want to visit Lindy, but a month from now or a year from now, you could decide that you want her to live with you."

"I swear I won't, Deke," Angie declared. "I wouldn't do that to you."

"I wouldn't let you do that to me," he in-formed her grimly. "A lot has been said about the way a mother will fight for her young, but a father will fight just as tenaciously for his. I'd advise you to remember that, Angie."

"I'll remember it." She finally faced him squarely. "But why should either of us fight? You aren't going to be able to keep me away from Lindy. Why should you even try? It's wrong for you to deprive Lindy of her mother's love—my love."

"Her mother's love." His mouth curved contemptuously. "A mother who abandoned her at birth—who had made no attempt to see her in seven years—who hadn't even held her child in her arms until today?"

Angie winced at his bitter truths. "That isn't the way I wanted it."

"Is that why you decided to 'use' lover boy to try to get Lindy?" Deke challenged. "Ever since I've known you, Angie, you've used people. Used them until you had satisfied whatever particular whim you had at the time. Then you just turned your back and forgot them. It was just tough luck if they happened to get hurt, wasn't it?"

"That isn't true!" Aghast, Angie stared at him.

"Isn't it?" he mocked. "You knew Teddy-boy wanted to go to bed with you, so you were going to use him to fight me. And what about today when you 'used' my sister to see Lindy? You don't really give a damn that you've ruined my relationship with Marissa—that I can't trust my own sister. No, you got to see Lindy so it was worth it. It didn't hurt you."

"It was wrong. I admit it." Angie felt small and wretched. "I don't think you realize how desperate I was to see Lindy. It's been building up inside me for seven years, Deke. And here I was so close to her."

"I'm not going to let you hurt Lindy," he stated.

"I don't want to hurt her," Angie argued. "I want to love her." She searched for a way to make him understand how much it meant to her to have her child again. "I've given up my job—probably my career—my own home, everything that I once thought was important, just so I can be near my daughter. Doesn't that show you how much I care?"

Deke studied her with a certain hard cynicism in his features. "It tells me you probably became tired of your career. Who's going to suffer? Not you. Your boss, temporarily, until he finds a replacement." He paused. "I know you, Angie."

"I don't think you understand me," she insisted on a heavy sigh.

"What is it this time, Angie? Do you want to experience maternal love? Is that why you're here?" he cross-examined her motives, then supplied his own deductive reasoning. "You wanted to experience sex and you used me for a partner. Unfortunately, you got pregnant. You wouldn't even consider an abortion, I suppose because you wanted to experience childbirth. But you weren't interested in raising a child. That would take too much of your time. So you decided you wanted the experience of a career, and pawned the baby off on me."

"You make me sound selfish and irresponsible. Seven years ago, I was scared and alone," Angie defended herself and fought back the tears.

"You weren't alone. I was there."

"You." Her short laugh was bitter. "You were just like everybody else." And none of them cared about her. "But it doesn't really matter what happened back then. This is today, and I want my child."

"You can't have Lindy," Deke stated. "If you want something to mother, then have another baby. I'm sure lover boy would be more than happy to get you pregnant."

"I can't." Angie lowered her chin, biting her lip at the stillness that followed her reply. She felt his sharpened attention. Then his hand was under her chin, raising it and forcing her to look at him.

"What do you mean—you can't?" Deke frowned. "Are you saying you can't have children? The doctor told me it was a normal delivery. He never mentioned any damage."

"There's no . . . physical problem." Angie averted her gaze from his face. It wasn't a subject she could talk about with ease, especially with him. "I just seem to . . . freeze up." Deke waited for her to elaborate. "About a year after the baby was born, I . . . went to the doctor to find out . . . what was wrong with me. He said it was normal for a woman to . . . lose interest in sex after the birth of a child. He assured me . . . it wouldn't last. But—"

"Are you saying that you haven't had sex with any man since the last time we made love?" Deke wanted her to be more explicit. The wonder in his voice bordered on skepticism.

Angie flashed him a hurt look of angry pride. "I'm not asking you to believe me," she said tightly and looked away. "I don't know— maybe I'm scared of getting pregnant. Or I have a guilty conscience because I gave away my baby. But I just can't—" The muscles in her throat constricted in pain, and she couldn't finish the sentence. Angie pressed her lips together, refusing to make any further attempt to convince Deke that what she said was true.

The roughness of his calloused thumb moved slowly over the outline of her mouth, rubbing the soft curves of her lips.

"You're right," Deke acknowledged. "I find it hard to believe."

Even though she expected his doubt, it still stabbed her. Closing her eyes, she breathed in sharply and caught the manly smell of him, virile and warm. Awareness shivered along her nerve ends at how closely he was standing to her. His thumb continued its absorbing study of her mouth, a disturbing sensuality entering his touch.

"You enjoyed making love, Angie." The pitch of his voice had deepened to a husky level, an edge of reluctance in it as if it was something he didn't want to recall. "Do you remember the first time we made love?" His fingers curved themselves against her neck while his thumb trailed slowly across her cheek to her ear. "We took the boat into the Gulf and dropped anchor to laze on the deck in the sun."

"Yes." She opened her eyes to look at him, stimulated by his words and his touch. The blue of her eyes had darkened to a midnight hue, a longing burned in them to recapture the enchantment of that afternoon seven years ago. *"The Southern Breeze,"* Angie murmured the name of the boat.

"Yes," Deke confirmed the accuracy of her memory as his gaze fathomed the deep blue of her eyes. "There was just you and I, and a bottle of suntan lotion. You started out rubbing it over my shoulders and back, massaging it in."

Angie quivered with the sensation of his hard flesh beneath her hands, all male sinew and bone. The lotion had given her a heady excuse to leisurely explore his body, to feel the rippling muscles of his arms and the solid flatness of his stomach. Of their own volition, her hands spread themselves across his chest, feeling the heat generated by his body through the thin material of his white shirt. It intensified the memory of his sun-warmed flesh.

"Then it was my turn to spread the lotion over you," Deke murmured thickly, and Angie quivered as his hand traveled slowly down her neck and pushed the collar of her robe aside to expose the creamy gold of a bare shoulder.

They were both trapped in the spell of the past, caught in the vortex of remembered passion. It smouldered anew, flicking through Angie's veins with a disturbing heat. There was a hand at her back, drawing her a few inches closer before it moved to push the robe off her other shoulder. She was having difficulty breathing normally, her pulse racing away with itself.

"You were wearing a skimpy blue bikini that already had my imagination working overtime." Deke lowered his gaze to the vicinity of her breasts still partially hidden from his view by the robe. The almost physical touch of his gaze seemed to make them strain against the confinement of the terrycloth material. "It was a simple matter to untie the halter strings." As Deke reminded her of his action that day, his fingers loosened the knot of the cloth belt that held the robe in place.

The overlapping front of the robe swung open, causing Angie to take a quick breath that became lodged in her throat. It was released in a shuddering sigh when his hand cupped the weight of a naked breast in its palm. Then his mouth drifted onto hers and her lips parted under the first pressure.

The kiss grew hard and hungry, ravenous in its desire for satisfaction. Angie dissolved under the melting force of Deke's ardor, offering no resistance when his hands pulled the robe from her body and her nude form was gathered against his male length. Timeless sensations swirled through her system, heating her flesh with age-old needs. His roaming hands fitted her to the rangy contours of his body, the coarse denim of his Levis abrasive against her sensitized bare hips and legs.

The compulsion was strong to feel his flesh against her skin. It guided her fingers to the buttons of his shirt, unfastening them to slip her hands inside and rediscover the rippling muscles contracting under his skin at her touch. Then Deke was aiding her, pulling his shirt free of the waistband to give her unlimited contact with his hair-roughened chest and stomach. His tongue licked into the secret recesses of her mouth, finally filling it and mating with hers.

Nothing existed—not time or place. All that Angie knew was that she was enclosed in the familiar intimacy of his embrace. Her insides were knotted with sweet agony, aching to absorb him into her flesh, to have him fill the emptiness that throbbed for him. She dug her fingers into his shoulders in a silent demand. A muffled sound came from his throat as Deke dragged his mouth from hers. He was breathing hard, little beads of perspiration forming above his upper lip. When he looked down at her eagerly trembling body, he seemed to be warring within himself.

"It's no use," Deke muttered at last and swung her off the floor and into his arms. "I've got to have you."

His mouth was on hers again, not allowing time for second thoughts or for Angie to take in the full impact of what was happening. Carrying her to the bed, Deke laid her down and stripped out of his clothes. Angie watched him, aware that his eyes were taking in every female inch of her and sending a fire coursing through her veins. She had never belonged to anyone else but him. When he came to the bed, she knew she had never wanted to belong to anyone else but Deke.

For a second, she was frozen by the realization, then the mattress sagged under his additional weight. Angie ceased to be conscious of anything but the virile body pressed next to her. His mouth was on her lips, eating them only to be sidetracked by the delectable curve of her throat and later the swelling thrust of her breast. All the while, his hands roamed over her body, manipulating and exciting Angie to a point of frenzy. She strained toward him, seeking the gratification his hard manhood promised.

"Love me, Deke," she moaned when it seemed she was going to die from wanting him.

With a groan, he rolled on top of her, sliding between her legs and pinning her to the mattress with his weight. She barely managed to bite back the sharp cry of pain at his entrance. It had been so long that it hurt as if it were the first time all over again, but there was pleasure in the pain, a pleasure that grew and expanded until it swelled and burst in a golden rush of fire. It consumed them both, a raging fever that left them weak—and wholly satisfied.

Lying in his arms with her head nestled on his chest, Angie listened to the solid beat of his heart and enjoyed the enfolding warmth of his arms. Her body tingled with leftover pleasure, tired and content at last. She closed her eyes, soothed by steady rise and falls of his chest, and the fact that Deke had made no move to leave her.

Outside the sun had gone down and night was closing in. Sleep stole languidly over her. Just before Angie lost consciousness, she was dimly aware of Deke pulling a cover over them. It was the last thing she remembered before she drifted off.

Sometime in the night, Angie stirred and encountered an arm of resistence when she tried to move. She was shocked into wakefulness by the discovery that someone was in bed with her—a man. She was lying on her side and a distinctly male body was molded to her shape, a large hand possessively holding her breast. For a split second, her memory was blank and an instinct to escape the stranger's hold prodded her to move. The instant the arm tightened around her again to keep Angie in his embrace, she remembered it was Deke and her stiffness subsided.

"Where do you think you're going?" he growled sleepily near her ear.

"Nowhere—now," she softly added the last.

"Then come back here." His hand glided down her stomach and pressed to fit her again to the curve of his lean hips. The casual intimacy was more than her senses could handle. Somehow her awareness was transmitted to Deke. "Something wrong?"

Her muscles were tensing with excitement as his hand lingered familiarly near her legs. "I'm used to sleeping alone," Angie whispered.

"So I discovered," Deke murmured and nuzzled the hair along her neck. "Are you sore?"

"A little," she admitted and tried to ignore the faint tremors within. "I didn't mean to disturb you." Now that he was awake, he might leave and Angie was just beginning to enjoy the idea of sleeping with him.

His hand shifted back to her breast and immediately became motionless. Angie didn't understand the reason for his sudden stillness until his thumb rolled around the hardened point of an aroused nipple. She was left in no doubt of his reaction when Deke stiffened in response.

"You've disturbed me ever since the day we met," he declared with sudden briskness. "That hasn't changed." In the very next second, he was rolling her onto her back. He loomed above her. "Damn you for making me want you, Angie." Then everything was blotted out by the fierce possession of his kiss, demanding that she give all he wanted to take. And Angie had never been able to deny him anything he wanted.

The telephone jangled a second time before the sound penetrated Angie's exhausted sleep. Only this time when she awakened, she didn't have to wonder whose arm was around her. She knew it belonged to Deke. Moving as little as possible so she wouldn't waken him, Angie reached out a hand and picked up the receiver. She glanced at Deke, dark lashes still closed in sleep. His chiseled, male features were relaxed, their innate strength tugging at her heart.

"Hello." She spoke in a very low voice, thick with sleep.

"Is that you, Angie?" Since she had expected to hear Ted's voice on the other end of the line, she was surprised to recognize Marissa.

"Yes." Angie stiffened in sudden apprehension.

"Deke had the name of this motel written down, but the manager kept insisting you weren't registered. I was practically out of my mind before it hit me that you probably hadn't used your own name." She sounded frantic. "I just had to talk to you before Deke comes in."

"What's wrong, Marissa? Is it Lindy?" Angie's first thought was that something had happened to her daughter.

The receiver was taken out of her hand before she heard the answer. Deke was awake and had commandeered the phone, its cord stretching across her. "What is it, Marissa?" he asked while Angie scanned his face anxiously.

"Is Lindy all right?" she whispered and was relieved when Deke nodded, smiling at her briefly.

"What was that? I didn't quite catch what you said," he directed his reply to the phone, although he continued to look at Angie. "I guess I'm not awake yet."

Assured now that Lindy was well, Angie became self-conscious when she realized Deke had admitted he'd spent the night with her. To her, it was still something very private. She wasn't sure if she was ready for his sister to know, but it was too late. Deke had already intimated as much.

"No, it doesn't," Deke said in response to a comment from Marissa. "What time is it?" There was a pause, then his mouth crooked. "That late, huh?" He levered himself onto an elbow, facing Angie. "Tell Lindy I'll be home around noon. We'll talk then." He reached across her to hang up the phone, then stayed partially leaning over her when it was done. There was something hooded about his steady look, something that made his expression unreadable. It made her uneasy, a sensation that didn't entirely go away, even when his hand stroked her cheek in a light caress.

"Why did Marissa call?" Angie asked when it appeared Deke wasn't going to tell her.

He caught at a lock of tawny blond hair and watched it slide through his fingers. "She was worried about you," he replied in an absent tone. When his glance returned to her face, there was a wry lift to one side of his mouth. "She knew I was angry when I came here last night. I suppose she thought I might harm you in some way. Now she knows differently."

"I see," she murmured inadequately and avoided his gaze, focusing her attention on the brawny width of his bare chest, tanned and muscled.

"Does it bother you that my sister knows we slept together last night?" Deke guessed at the reason for her reticence.

"A little," Angie admitted, because she didn't know what it meant. No commitment had been made. Was it something that had happened because of their past affair? Had it merely been an act of gratifying sexual urges? Or did the cause run deeper? Angie was reluctant to ask Deke—just as she was reluctant to delve into her own heart. Whatever was in it was too fragile at the moment to endure a cold examination.

"It isn't as if we never knew each other before last night," Deke mocked her lightly.

"I know," she murmured and pushed aside the covers to climb out of bed. Deke didn't try to keep her there.

But he questioned, "Are you getting up now?" By implication, he was suggesting there was another activity they could pursue.

Without looking at him, she ignored his subtle invitation to return to the bed and his arms. "It's late." She was much too self-conscious with him—too vividly aware of his eyes on her. She was worried that he might guess a secret that she herself didn't know. In the center of the room, Angie paused to pick up her robe from the floor and slip it on before continuing to the bathroom.

When Angie left the bed, Deke leaned back on the pillow and cradled his head with his hands. He watched her walk away, a graceful nude—slim and shapely—female beauty in its natural form and he wanted to possess her, but he restrained that hot desire.

If Marissa hadn't called, he might have been tempted—but she had phoned. Deke had known his sister would call if she had the opportunity. He had known it last night. Angie hadn't. She hadn't even guessed. There was no sense of triumph—no satisfaction in successfully intercepting the call. Deke stopped pretending it was the reason he'd stayed all night, instead of leaving after he'd made love to Angie the first time.

His blood was stirred by the sight of Angie's softly rounded hips and the jutting angle of her firm breasts. When she disappeared inside the bathroom, Deke faced the bitter truth at last. He hadn't gotten her out of his system. He was still hooked on her and he despised himself for being so weak.

Swinging his feet out of bed, he sat up on the edge and reached for the jockey shorts and

Levis on the floor. His mind was already working on the plan that had been taking shape all night long. Deke didn't attempt to justify the rightness of it or the fairness—not even to himself.

Leaning over the sink, Angie cupped her hands under the running tap water and splashed it on her face to rinse off the soap. She repeated the process twice more and turned off the water. As she reached for the towel to dry her face, she thought she heard a knock at the motel room door. She heard the door open and guessed that Deke had answered it.

An instant later, he called for her. "Angie! It's for you."

With the towel in hand, Angie opened the bathroom door and stepped into the room. Her questioning glance ran first to Deke, clad only in his Levis. He was barefoot, standing by the door. Amusement glittered dryly in his gray eyes.

"There she is." He half-turned to address the man in the doorway. "Without even a scratch or a bruise." Then Deke was once again looking at Angie, but she was staring at Ted's grim expression. "Mr. Sullivan insisted on seeing for himself that you were unharmed."

In silent accusation, Ted looked from Angie's semi-decently clad figure to the bed that showed obvious signs of being slept in by two people. The glance he turned on Deke was filled with bitter loathing. Anyone with half an eye could see that Deke had just gotten up. His dark hair was rumpled from sleep and there was the shadow of a night's growth on his lean cheeks. Angie's face was warm with self-consciousness at the knowledge that burned in Ted's eyes.

"Hello, Ted." She moved hesitantly toward the door, aware that Deke seemed to be absently amused by her discomfort.

"I tried to call, but your line was busy." His look seemed to imply they'd taken the phone off the hook.

Before Angie could respond, Deke moved away from the door and paused when he reached her. "If you're through in the bathroom, honey, I'll get cleaned up." He said it so casually, as if they'd lived together for years, when in actuality they never had. Her heart did a funny little somersault at the easy endearment.

"You can use it," she said, even though she still had to put her makeup on and brush her hair.

But Deke didn't go on by her as she expected him to do. He framed her face with his hands and tilted it. His branding kiss seared her lips as his own, leaving little doubt that he reguarded her as his possession. It left her shaken, a fact Deke noted when he raised his head.

"Get rid of him, honey." His voice was low. The affectionate term was all that saved it from being an order. Angie wasn't sure she liked the confident expression carved in his features. In the next second, Deke had released her and was striding toward the bathroom.

She hesitated briefly, glancing at Ted. He was angry and upset. She walked to the door, trying to think of something to say and coming up blank.

"I guess I don't have to ask if you're all right," Ted declared on an irritated note. "It's obvious you won't be needing my help anymore."

"I don't know." Which was the truth. Angie didn't know what all this meant any more than Ted did.

He appeared to catch the sincerity in her voice and his gaze narrowed to study her. "Angie, did he force you to go to bed with him? I don't necessarily mean physically."

In all honesty, she had to admit, "No, he didn't force me."

"He strikes me as the type who could be ruthless." Ted didn't try to conceal his dislike. "I wouldn't have put it past him to use your daughter to get you into his bed."

"Well, that isn't what happened." Angie didn't attempt to deny Ted's claim because she wasn't sure how well she knew Deke. Wasn't he still a stranger? A stranger she knew intimately, but a stranger just the same. Yet, that wasn't entirely true either. Deke was the father of her child. He had shown honor in marrying her seven years ago, and later, responsibility in assuming the care of their daughter. In addition, Deke possessed an inner strength and a keen intelligence. There were many qualities about him to admire. But this knowledge seemed to confuse her more. It was little wonder that Ted couldn't understand.

"I guess there's nothing to keep me here this weekend," Ted concluded, but waited for her to refute it.

"Thank you . . . for coming," Angie offered instead.

He sighed heavily in a disgruntled anger. "I thought I was too smart to be made into a fool by a woman."

"That isn't true, Ted," Angie denied. "Don't feel that way."

"How am I supposed to feel when I know it could have been me in that bed this morning?" he argued.

His assertion angered her. "If it could have been, you would have been in it before this morning. But you haven't been, have you?" she challenged, and Ted shifted uncomfortably. Stiffly polite, Angie continued. "I appreciate the help you've given me—and I hope you have a safe trip back to Houston."

Ted hesitated, then mumbled a terse, "Good-bye, Angie . . ." and walked away.

Regret mixed with her anger as she closed the door and leaned against it. She had the oddest sensation of being watched and looked up to find Deke studying her from the bath-room doorway, a towel in his hands. She straightened under his measuring look.

"I don't think he'll be back," Deke re-marked, and he resumed wiping his hands and arms on the towel.

"No, he's left for Houston." Which wasn't what Deke was talking about, but Angie chose not to agree that she wouldn't be seeing Ted again.

Wadding the towel into a ball, Deke turned and tossed it inside the bathroom. "Better get dressed."

"I will." Angie started toward the closet.

"Then you can pack."

She stopped, a few feet from him. Without a razor, Deke hadn't shaved, but his dark hair was combed in a semblance of order. "What did you say?"

"I said you could pack when you're dressed," he repeated his statement, his smooth expression showing no variance. Angie could only stare at him, not certain what that portended. There was a lazy curve to the line of his mouth. "You don't think I'm going to let you stay in this place, do you?"

She couldn't help being wary and a little suspicious despite their recent closeness. "Deke, if you think I'm going to leave and not see Lindy—"

"Did I say anything about that?" Deke mocked her, but Angie couldn't see what was in his eyes. Their metallic color shielded his inner thoughts.

"Then where—"

A long, easy stride brought him to her side. His hands settled on her shoulders. "You'll see," he assured her and turned her toward the closet, giving her a little push. "Get dressed."

Chapter Eight

W hile Angie made one last check of the motel room to make certain she hadn't left anything, Deke carried her belongings outside. A few minutes later, she followed him. In the parking lot, she hesitated when she saw him stowing her things in the trunk of his car.

"Is that everything?" At her nod, he pushed the trunk lid shut and walked around to the driver's door. He noticed her hovering uncertainly and said, "We're taking my car."

"What about mine?" Angie frowned, because Deke still hadn't told her where they were going. "I can't leave it here."

"I'll have one of my men pick it up," he replied, and he opened the door on the driver's side to slide behind the wheel.

After another uneasy glance at her car, Angie walked to the passenger side of his car and climbed in beside him. His gray glance touched her briefly, telling her no secrets. Then he was starting the car and driving away from the motel. It was moments like these when Deke was silent and uncommunicative that made Angie uneasy with him. This was when she doubted that she knew him at all.

With sidelong looks, she studied him. The cut of his profile was strong and forceful—the clean line of his jaw and the forward thrust of his chin. His cheeks were tanned lean and hard, the skin stretching tautly over his cheekbones and grooves etched at the corners of his mouth. A hat covered the virile thickness of his dark hair and shaded those impenetrable gray eyes. Her glance strayed to his mouth, so lacking in softness yet so capable of passion. *Like his hands*—she thought, and studied the work-roughened hands on the wheel. They were a man's hands, firm in their grip and always in control whether it was controlling this car at fast speeds or controlling her.

There was no conversation as Deke pointed the car south of Goliad. This was the way he'd been after Angie became pregnant seven years ago and they'd married. He had never talked to her, not about things that mattered. He had never confided his feelings to her, nor asked how she felt. When Angie had tried to express her thoughts to him, Deke had usually brushed them aside with the phrase that had become meaningless from repetition—"We'll work it out." That's when Angie had come up with her own solution for the situation that had become impossible.

Had anything changed?

Sighing inwardly, Angie turned her gaze out the window. The countryside was rough and broken, thick with scrub brush and mesquite and creased with dry washbeds. The autumn grass was tall and pale brown, cured by a Texas sun. Occasionally, Angie had glimpses of cattle lazing in the shade of live oaks.

The closer they got toward the Gulf Coast, the terrain changed into a mixture of marshy pastures and cotton fields. They passed a smattering of natural gas wells and the grasshopper-headed pumps of an oil well or two. Live oak trees began to dominate the landscape. Every now and then a house yard would have a citrus tree, its branches heavy with yellow or gold fruit.

When Deke turned onto the highway to Rockport, Angie couldn't contain her curiosity any longer. "Where are we going?" she asked again.

"Wait and see." Deke refused to enlighten her. "We'll be there soon enough."

Within minutes after they'd entered the city limits of Rockport, Deke took the road that slanted away from the highway along the Ski Basin. Angie instantly guessed their destination.

"You're taking me out on the Key," she said.

"We aren't using the summer house," Deke confirmed her guess that he was taking her to the Spanish-styled home. "It's just standing empty."

Her feelings were mixed as they approached the house. There were so many memories attached to the place, but Angie wasn't sure she wanted to live in the past. The clock couldn't be turned back, she realized, and everyone lived with memories. But she still wasn't sure why Deke had brought her here and he wasn't in the habit of explaining his actions.

Deke parked the car in the driveway and climbed out. He was walking to the front door when Angie stepped out of her side. She didn't hurry to catch up with him, letting her gaze wander over the white stuccoed walls and the tiled roof. She had always liked the house and fantasized about living there herself. Maybe that was what bothered her more than the memories associated with it.

When she reached the front entrance, Deke had the door unlocked and was waiting for her before going inside. "It's been shut up since August." His glance was brief as he pushed the door open and moved to one side to allow Angie to enter first. "It will need to be aired."

The ground floor of the house was used mainly as a storage area because of the risk of high water. The living quarters were on the second floor, access was provided by a wide staircase. As Angie moved to the steps, the stale, stuffy air pressed its suffocating weight on her. She was conscious of Deke climbing the steps behind her, his firm tread echoing after her own.

At the top of the stairs, there was another door which was also locked. They brushed shoulders as Angie moved out of the way so Deke could unlock it. The physical contact sent a disturbing wave of sensation through her body. It was crazy how his touch had always been able to do that to her.

"You'll need the key," he said and handed it to her.

Her fingers closed around the warm metal, its notched edges poking into her palm. Angie looked up and found Deke studying her with a silent intensity. He seemed to hold her gaze for a long time as the blood pounded in her heart, but it was really only seconds. Without a word, he turned and pushed the door the rest of the way open, then walked in ahead of her.

The interior was dark; all the drapes were pulled closed, shutting out the sunlight. Deke crossed the room, weaving around the ghostly white shapes, and tugged on the drape cord to let in some light. All the furniture was covered with dust protectors that reminded Angie of shrouds. Deke stripped aside the one on the bright cinnamon couch and another on a matching chair, and the room seemed to come to life. But he didn't continue with the task of stripping the covers from the furniture. Instead, he walked back to where Angie was standing.

"It's practically the same as when you were here," Deke stated. "You remember your way around, don't you?"

"Yes." She knew the kitchen was to her left and the bedrooms were to the right, but there was still some rediscovery to be done.

"I'll bring your things up from the car." He moved immediately away from her to the stairs.

With the sound of his footsteps traveling swiftly down the steps, Angie looked around the room for a minute more, then the stale air became too oppressive. She crossed the room to the large windows facing the Gulf and unfastened the catch to slide them open. A fresh, salt breeze swept into the room to chase out the old air. She turned back to the room and looked at the two pieces of exposed furniture among the white mounds. Immediately, she set to work dragging off the rest of the white cloths on the other furniture and piled the covers in a heap to be folded later.

From the living room, Angie moved to the dining room, opening windows as she went. Engrossed in her task, she didn't hear Deke return and wasn't aware he was back until she turned and saw him standing in the archway watching her. She was surprised by something in his expression, but it was masked before she could read it. His glance made a sweeping inspection of the room, then came back to her.

"You've been busy," he remarked, and moved toward her with lithe ease. "But you always were able to stir things up in a hurry, weren't you?" Deke didn't seem to expect a reply. "I put your things in my room."

Something in the rich timbre of his voice reached out for her, although he made no attempt to touch her. Angie was laced with the feeling that he wasn't telling her everything.

"Why did you bring me here, Deke?" She searched his face for an answer, but it offered none.

"You want to be close to the ranch so you can see Lindy, don't you?" he replied smoothly.

"Yes," she nodded slowly.

"What could be more convenient than this house?" Deke reasoned. "It's completely furnished and no one's living in it. Which reminds me—I'm sure the cupboards are bare." He reached in his pocket and took out a money clip, peeling off some bills and handing them to her. "You'll need grocery money," he explained.

"I—" Angie wasn't sure she should accept it. First he'd given her a place to live; now he was offering her money for food.

His hands took hold of her shoulders and pulled her closer. "I have to get out to the ranch," he said, ignoring her attempted protest. His fingers tunneled into the hair by her ear while he ran his gaze over her features. "Have dinner ready at seven-thirty tonight."

Angie was still trying to sort through her confusion when Deke kissed her, his mouth firm and demanding in its possession. Disarmed completely by his expert invasion, she responded openly, but the scrape of his beard soon had her pulling away, her fingers touching the tender underside of her lip.

"I promise to shave." His mouth quirked in a lazy smile, then Deke was leaving her.

For several seconds, Angie stayed where she was, a little too numbed to move. She listened to his footsteps descending the stairs. An inner force compelled her to go to the head of the stairs. Deke was on the last step. He paused and looked up, as if sensing she was there. Suddenly Angie had to fill the silence.

"Give my love to Lindy," she said.

Something hard and unpleasant flashed in his eyes, then he was gone out of her sight without acknowledging her words. She felt chilled and hurt, and tried to convince herself that she had only imagined that look.

What was left of the morning went quickly as Angie busied herself with opening the house. She reexplored the house and its rooms, already familiar to her from previous visits with Marissa. There were minor changes, specifically in the bedrooms. Originally, one had been a guestroom; Deke and Marissa had each had a room of their own; and the master bedroom had belonged to their parents. The guest bedroom and Marissa's remained the same, but Deke's old room now contained a collection of stuffed toys, its mas-

culine decor changed to suit a little girl. Angie
took her time cleaning Lindy's room, polish-
ing the furniture and arranging the stuffed
toys. It was easy to tell which toy had been
Lindy's favorite. Angie picked up a dog-eared
kangaroo that was slightly dirty and worn
from much handling. She held it, pressing it
against her cheek for a few poignant seconds,
then returned it to its place with the other
toys.

With his parents' death, Deke had moved
into the master bedroom. It was one room
Angie had never been in and it was there that
Deke had left her clothes. The master suite
was typically large, with a sitting area in
addition to the queen-sized bed and its furniture. A sliding glass door opened onto a private balcony with a view of the blue Gulf
waters. The bathroom contained a shower
stall as well as a full-length tub, double sinks
and a dressing room. All the furnishings in the
suite were done in a deep marine blue with an
accent of gold, contrasting with the rooms'
white walls.

There was nearly as much floor space in the
bedroom suite as her apartment's living room
and bedroom had contained. Angie unpacked
her clothes and hung them in one of the two
walk-in closets. They looked almost forgotten
in the huge closet.

By the middle of the afternoon, Angie had
worked her way to the kitchen. It was ultra-
modern, with a center-island workspace and

every modern convenience imaginable. After taking stock of the supplies on hand, Angie began making a list of the groceries she'd need to buy. She heard a car pull into the driveway and stop. When she went to the window to look, a cowboy climbed out of her car and trotted to the road where a man in a pickup truck was waiting to give him a ride. Deke had her car delivered as promised.

By seven o'clock that evening, she had managed to make the house presentable, done the grocery shopping, taken a bath, changed clothes and had dinner on the stove. Angie was definitely proud of herself as she shredded lettuce into a salad bowl. She had always been organized, but she'd never had an occasion to test her domestic talents. She caught herself humming and realized she hadn't been this content in a long time.

A car drove in just as she was about to set the table. Angie glanced at the kitchen clock which showed a quarter past seven. If it was Deke, he was early. She heard a car door slam. Had it been one door or two? Angie lifted her head and looked toward the staircase, listening. Her heart gave a crazy little leap at the sound of a little girl's laugh. Quickly, she set the dinner plates on the counter and started toward the stair door.

Deke was almost to the top of the stairs when she reached the door. He paused a split second, then flashed her a smile that knocked her heart backward. Angie glanced behind him, expecting to see Lindy, but there was no one else. Frowning slightly, she searched the base of the stairs, then returned her gaze to Deke.

"I never guessed you'd be waiting at the door to welcome me," Deke murmured, a possessvie glitter in his eyes.

"Where's Lindy?" Angie saw the light fade and an impenetrable iron color take its place.

"What made you think I'd bring her?" His features were bland, his voice too casual. "I didn't say anything about it."

"No," Angie admitted. "It's just that—right after I heard the car drive in, I heard a little girl laughing. I thought it was Lindy."

"It must have been one of the neighbor's kids," he dismissed the subject and took hold of her arm to turn her out of the doorway. He let it stay around her as he followed her into the living quarters. "Is dinner ready? Something smells good."

"Almost. I still have to set the table."

The dinner should have been enjoyable. The food was good and the conversation flowed easily between them, but a seed of suspicion kept nagging at Angie. If she and Deke were getting along so well, why did he keep avoiding the subject of their daugher?

As Deke finished his coffee, Angie stood up to take the plates to the kitchen. "Leave the dishes till later," he said. "Let's go in the living room."

"All right." She found no reason to argue with his suggestion.

It was dark in the living room. While Deke turned on the lamp by the couch, Angie crossed over to the windows and closed the drapes. When she turned to face him, Deke was reclining on the couch with the coffee table acting as a footstool. The lamp cast a pool of light that masked his features in shadows. He appeared relaxed, yet steadily watchful.

Unable to bear the suspense of not knowing, Angie voiced the question that had hammered at the corners of her mind all through dinner. "When are you going to let me see Lindy?"

There was a long, stretching silence before Deke finally said, "Come here, Angie."

Her hesitation was slight before she walked to the couch. It was difficult to conduct a conversation with the width of the room dividing them. Deke swung his feet off the coffee table as though to give her access to the couch cushions next to him. But when Angie started to pass, he reached out to stop her, spreading his hand against the back of her thigh. Warmth radiated out from his touch, heating her flesh in spite of her efforts to retain control of her senses. She looked down and felt herself being drawn toward the silver brilliance of his gaze.

"Before we bring Lindy into this, we need to get to know each other," Deke told her. "Agreed?"

There was some logic in his statement—at least on his side. He had already indicated a lack of trust in her promise not to try to take Lindy from him.

"Agreed," she gave in reluctantly, although it did explain why he'd brought her here and why he'd come back for dinner.

His hand slid suggestively up her thigh to her rounded bottom. He applied pressure to pull her toward him while he caught at her hand. "Sit down." But Deke meant on his lap.

A spreading weakness lowered her resistance and she let herself be drawn onto his lap. Deke settled her comfortably against him, the seductive darkness of his eyes playing havoc with her pulse. When he moved to kiss her, Angie turned away at the last second and his mouth grazed her cheek. He nibbled at an earlobe and nuzzled the shell-like opening, sending quivers over her flesh. Her fingers curled into the material of his shirt, hanging on against his attempt to arouse her.

"Don't you think we should talk so we can get to know each other?" Angie suggested with throaty effort.

"We've been talking all through dinner, ever since I got here," Deke answered against her neck, his mouth warm and stimulating on her sensitive skin. His hand slid under her knit top and her stomach constricted sharply at the contact of his hand to her flesh. "I want to know all of you."

His hand continued its wayward journey up her ribcage, overriding Angie's mute objections, but it stopped when it encountered the obstacle of her brassiere. He slipped his hand behind her to the fastener. He lifted his head, his eyes three-quarter lidded while he viewed the weak protest written in her expression.

"Aren't you one of those liberated women who've eliminated the bra from their lingerie?" he chided, and watched the small gasp part her lips when he undid the hook to loosen the lacy cups encircling her breasts.

"No. It's uncomfortable without one," she managed a disturbed explanation.

"Then wear it in the daytime if you must." His hand was back in the front, working on a strap under the cover of her knit top. "But take it off at night so I won't have to fight with it."

His request barely registered at first. She was distracted by his hand. "What are you doing?"

"Releasing the straps." By then, Deke had detached the adjustable straps from the cups. He removed the disassembled bra without Angie having to take off her top. When the bra was tossed to some distant point on the living room floor, his hand once again slid under her top and closed on a rounded breast, kneading it with practiced ease.

Sensation was trying to swamp her, but Angie resisted it. His previous comment returning to mind. "Do you mean you'll be coming here at night?"

"I can't get to know you very well if I'm not around, can I?" he reasoned smoothly.

"No." She supposed it made sense, but she couldn't think any more.

He seemed to know it as he lifted her top and exposed her breasts for his visual and sensual enjoyment, caressing, kissing and teasing them until she melted. There was a shifting of positions until they were both lying on the couch and the hard pressure of his body was against hers.

Again, Deke pulled back to look at her, leaving her aching. "God, you're like a habit-forming drug, Angie," he muttered roughly. "I can only make it so long without a fix."

She didn't like being compared to a narcotic. It made her sound like something bad. She levered herself partially into a sitting position, but the hand on her bare waist kept her from getting too far away from him.

"You make it sound like I'm a sickness," she accused.

He didn't deny it. "It's hell wanting you, honey." He curved his hand over a firmly swollen breast. "Come make me feel good." His voice was thick with longing.

Angie swayed toward him and that was all it took.

It was a long time later before Deke carried her into the master suite. He joined her in bed and they made love again. She fell asleep in his arms.

When she woke up the next morning, Deke was in the shower. She laid in bed without moving, deliciously tired and content. There was a warm, wonderful glow inside her and

she didn't want to move in case it went away.
The shower water stopped running and Angie
listened to the noises he made in the dressing
room. When he emerged, fully dressed and
clean-shaven, he looked vitally handsome and
strong.

"Come on, sleepyhead." Deke saw she was
awake. "It's late. The coffee should be done.
You can fix me some breakfast."

Stretching catlike, she climbed out of bed
and padded to the bathroom. When she came
out, Deke had left the room. She dressed
quickly and went to the kitchen where she
found him sitting on a stool drinking freshly
perked coffee.

"What do you want for breakfast?" Angie
poured herself a cup of the coffee and set it on
the island counter.

"Bacon and eggs, soft scrambled." Deke put
in his order.

"Toast?"

"Right."

Doubling the portions, she fixed herself the
same and sat down at the counter bar to eat
breakfast with him. When they had finished,
she cleared away the plates and stacked them
in the sink. She paused beside the percola-
tor.

"More coffee?" she asked as she unplugged
it to carry the pot to the counter where their
cups were.

"Just half a cup. I've got to be going," Deke
reminded her.

A faint smile touched her mouth as she filled his cup half full. "I feel like a wife getting her husband off to work."

It became very quiet for a minute. Angie glanced at Deke. His expression was grim and withdrawn. He flicked her a cutting look that seemed to slice right to the quick.

"We never did get around to being husband and wife, did we?" It was a biting retort. "It's a pity you never gave us a chance, Angie. We might have been able to make it work."

He didn't bother to drink the coffee she'd poured him. Instead, Deke pushed off the stool and walked toward the staircase. The warm glow had been blown out by his chilling rejoinder. Angie had no defense against his observation, nothing she could say in her own behalf. He paused at the door to take his hat from the hook.

"I should be here by seven for dinner," he informed her.

"Okay." But she doubted that Deke heard her, his footsteps on the stairs drowning out her reply.

The pattern had been set for the following week. Deke would come for dinner and stay the night, rising early in the morning and having Angie fix him breakfast. They talked about a lot of things, but never Lindy or the past. They made love. In many respects,

Angie had the feeling she was leading the life of a married woman. What was a little more frightening was the knowledge that she was liking it. It was so easy to remember that they had been married—and so easy to forget that they weren't.

Chapter Nine

*M*usic was playing softly in the background; the only light in the living room came from the lamp by the couch where Angie was curled contentedly in Deke's arms. His feet were propped on the coffee table while her legs were stretched across the couch cushions. His hand absently fingered her amber silk hair. These quiet moments in the evening had become part of their pattern, too.

Angie's thoughts wandered ahead. "I suppose you'll be spending Thanksgiving with Lindy," she murmured, which was only three days away.

"Why?" Deke responded with a question.

"Sometime soon I'm going to have to drive to Houston to move my things out of the apartment. The Thanksgiving holidays might be a perfect time to do it," she explained. "It's no fun being alone anyway on a holiday, so I might as well go."

"How long will it take?" Deke neither agreed nor objected to her suggestion, but he also didn't deny that she would be alone.

"I can drive up Thursday. I'll have to be there on Friday to close my bank accounts. Depending on how long it takes me to pack and load everything in the car, I should be able to leave Saturday to come back," Angie replied, thinking out loud.

"I have tickets for the Dallas game, so I'll probably be gone, too." He was taking it for granted that she was making the trip.

There seemed no reason not to after his statement. Angie noticed that Deke didn't ask her to go with him. She had no part in his life outside this house.

"I'll go then," she decided. "I'll leave early Thursday morning and hopefully miss some of the holiday traffic."

"Okay."

"Deke." She knew he wasn't going to like it but she had to ask anyway. "Doesn't Lindy wonder where you spend your nights?" Angie felt the ripple of impatience that went through him.

"No. Why should she? Most of the time she's getting ready for bed when I leave," he replied with a faint terseness.

"And Marissa?"

"If my sister has guessed, she knows better than to mention it to me. It isn't any of her business where I go or what I do."

"But if something happened to Lindy—"

"They can call me. I've left the phone number." His fingers tightened in her hair, tugging at the roots to pull her head back so he could see her face. There was suppressed anger in the hard line of his jaw. "Are you trying to remind me of my duty? Or are you tired of having me around again?"

"No—to both," Angie retorted in hurt defense. "I was just curious."

"It's a damned good thing you said no." Deke crushed her mouth under his, punishing her with hard kisses that were meant to bruise.

Angie tasted blood in her mouth where he had ground her lips against her teeth. Then he was prying them open to sensually lick away the hurt and wipe away the taste. His half-angry love offered her a release from her own frustration and she turned fully into his arms.

Gazing at the assortment of clothes, household wares, linens and a hundred other things, Angie wondered how she was going to pack it all. She doubted if she had enough boxes, and even then, she didn't know if it would all fit in her car.

With a sigh, Angie walked into the small

bedroom to change out of the dress she'd worn to the bank. At least she had that much accomplished. Her bank accounts were closed and she had a cashier's check for the balance in her purse. Between going to the bank and stopping at the office where she had worked to pick up her final paycheck and say goodbye to her co-workers, the morning had been shot. On impulse, she had phoned Ted's office, but his secretary wasn't expecting him in over the holidays. Angie wasn't sure why she had called him except—it seemed the decent thing to do.

An old sweatshirt and a faded pair of jeans waited on the unmade bed. Once her dress was off and on a hanger, she put them on and went back to the living room to tackle the chore of packing. She seemed to have amassed an endless array of knick-knacks and breakables. Angie carefully wrapped each one with newspaper and fitted them in boxes, trying to use every inch of space.

The knock on her door brought a sigh of irritation from Angie. It was probably the landlord since he had to inspect the apartment for any possible damage or theft before returning her deposit. The place was a mess. He would probably dock her for cleaning costs. Scrambling to her feet, she made her way through the maze of boxes to the door and tried to look pleasant when she opened the door.

But it was Ted standing in the hallway, not her landlord. "Hi," he smiled a little too brightly. "I checked in with the office and they mentioned you had stopped for your things. I thought I might find you here."

"Come in," Angie invited, but she realized she wasn't totally at ease with him anymore. "How have you been?"

"Fine." He walked in, glancing around. "You're busy packing I see."

"The place is a mess," she admitted. "I don't remember bringing half this much from Arizona."

"Then you're really leaving?" The inflection of his voice made it a question.

"Yes."

"I thought you might have changed your mind," he suggested.

"No." Angie felt awkward. "Would you like some coffee? I'm afraid all I have is instant."

"No thanks," Ted refused. "I just came by to see how you were." He hesitated, giving the impression that he might be uncomfortable, too. "When's the wedding?"

"Wedding?" Angie repeated.

"Didn't you and your ex get things patched up?" His interest sharpened when she avoided his look.

"I'm not sure." She didn't know how to describe her present relationship with Deke, but marriage had certainly not been discussed by either of them. She tried not to acknowledge to herself that the idea was appealing.

"That morning the two of you were real lovey-dovey," Ted reminded her needlessly.

"We haven't talked about getting married," Angie admitted, but didn't comment on his assessment of their attitude. That was the problem. Deke was her lover—and nothing more. An ache started to hurt someplace in her chest.

"Where will you be moving?" he asked, then inserted before she could answer. "Last week I called the motel where you were staying, but they said you left without a forwarding address."

"Deke has a summer house in Rockport. Since it's usually closed for the winter, he's letting me live in it." Angie moved away and pretended to organize a stack of linen in preparation for packing.

But Ted was too astute. "Alone?" he questioned.

Her cheeks reddened with embarrassment. "Not always," she admitted, but didn't tell him that Deke came every night.

"How convenient for him," he murmured caustically.

"Ted, I don't think—"

"—it's any of my business," Ted finished the sentence for her. "Maybe it isn't," he conceded. "But I can't help being concerned."

"That's kind of you, Ted, but—"

"I'm not sure how much kindness has to do with it." He smiled wryly. "I owe you an apology for the way I behaved the last time I saw you. I've always been a sore loser. And

I didn't exactly distinguish myself when I discovered you'd spent the night with him. It caught me completely off guard, and I felt I'd been let down. So I lashed out, trying to hurt you because I'd been hurt. I'm sorry, Angie."

"Apology accepted," she murmured. It served no purpose to remind him she hadn't given him any cause to feel that way.

"I feel better." His smile grew more natural. "What kind of agreement were you able to reach about your daughter?"

Angie reacted the way Deke usually did, trying to avoid the subject. "We haven't come to any final understanding," she hedged.

But it didn't slip past Ted. "He is letting you see her, isn't he?"

"Not yet," she admitted and hurried to ask, "Did you ever bother to look over the papers? The bank said you had stopped."

"You are staying in his house and he's 'visiting' you." He suggestively stressed the word. "But he hasn't permitted you to see your daughter. Angie, why did you ever agree to that?"

She began refolding the towels into smaller squares, anything to hide her inner turmoil and confusion. "Deke feels we should get to know each other again."

"My God, that's rich!" Ted laughed shortly, without humor. "He wants to 'know' you, huh? And you fell for it."

"You don't understand," she retorted in irritation. "Deke is worried that I will try to take Lindy away from him permanently."

"There isn't a chance of that and he knows it!" Ted declared. "That document has virtually signed, sealed and delivered your child into his exclusive care. I've never read anything so iron-tight. There isn't a loophole in it. There isn't even a pinhole in it. You only have the slimmest chance that a court might reverse it to the extent of granting you limited visiting privileges."

"You have studied it," she murmured and sagged against the armrest of the sofa. He made it sound hopeless.

"Yes. So did Sam." He tempered his voice to a less forceful level, knowing his news came as a blow to her. "I'm sorry, Angie."

"I think I knew it when Deke said the decision would ultimately rest with him." She stared at the towel that her fingers had wadded into a tight ball.

"Is that why you agreed to . . . his arrangement?" he inquired with new gentleness.

"It wasn't a question of agreeing to. It just happened," and she had found herself accepting it—not just accepting it, there was more involved, but she didn't want to think about that yet.

"Angie, he's just stringing you along. Your daughter is the carrot dangling in front of you. As long as he keeps her out of reach, he's got you where he wants you," Ted informed her sadly. "You're being used, Angie. Can't you see it?"

"He'll let me see her." She clung to that thought.

"Don't kid yourself," Ted insisted.

"I think I know him better than you do," Angie replied in defense.

"I'd bet you know him better." His comment was heavy with sexual innuendo, and Angie stiffened in outrage, flashing him an angry look. Ted ran a hand through his hair. "That remark was out of line. I'm sorry. . . . It's just that—" he paused. "Angie, are you in love with him?"

His question splintered through her, shattering the secret she'd kept locked away from herself. She had insisted for so long that her attraction to Deke was purely sexual, that she had finally believed it until now. She loved him. All along her feelings for him had been so simple that she hadn't understood them. Love was an emotion that didn't break down for analysis. It simply existed in its natural form.

Ted must have seen it in her face. "I guess that answers my question." He walked to the door and Angie was still too stunned by her discovery to leave. "Goodbye, Angie . . . and good luck."

The door had already clicked shut when she finally added, "Goodbye, Ted."

With new energy, she set to work. She couldn't pack fast enough, because she wanted to go home—home to Deke. She was certain he had some feelings for her that could be salvaged. They had a chance, she was sure.

All manner of things seemed to crop up to delay her. On Saturday morning, she had to wait for the landlord to inspect the apartment, so she had a late start. The traffic was heavy which slowed her down more. Then her car's radiator hose busted and she had to wait in Victoria for it to be repaired. It was late Saturday afternoon when she finally reached Rockport.

Her car was loaded to the gills so she didn't want to leave it in the driveway. Since she didn't want to take the time to unpack it, Angie parked it in the garage-half of the ground floor and locked the doors. The only thing she took out of the car was a suitcase of clothes. It wasn't six o'clock yet when she climbed the stairs. If Deke came, it wouldn't be until seven or after. Which gave her time to bathe and change into something more attractive than the travel-wrinkled pantsuit she was wearing.

She went straight to the master suite and left the suitcase unopened on the bed to enter the bathroom and turn on the faucets in the tub. While it filled with water, she returned to the bedroom and unlatched the suitcase. She shook out the aquamarine dress on top and laid it on the bed. Then it was back to the bathroom to add perfumed crystals of bubble bath to the water.

Angie didn't bother to turn on any lights

except the ones in the combination bath and dressing room. Bubbles billowed in the tub, fragrantly scented steam permeating the air as she undressed. She piled her blond hair on top of her head and secured it with a pair of combs. The tub was nearly full when she stopped at the linen closet for a towel and washcloth.

With the water running, she didn't hear a sound. Almost at the same second that Angie realized someone was behind her, a pair of arms circled her waist. She started to scream as she was gathered against a man's body and he buried his face in the curve of her neck. The scream never got past the sharply indrawn breath of alarm before Angie recognized the feel of those arms and that body.

"You're back," Deke murmured, and let her turn around.

There was raw hunger in his kiss that seemed to eat at her very soul. Angie strained close, pressing herself to his entire length, her arms wound tightly around his neck. The crush of his arms was an exquisite pain she could have endured for an endless time but he drew away. Angie lowered her gaze, not willing for him to see the love she guessed was in her eyes.

"I didn't hear you come in." There was a breathless quality to her voice. "I just got back a few minutes ago myself."

"The tub's going to overflow," Deke warned her with a faint smile.

Quickly, she slipped out of his arms to shut

off the faucets. Water was already gurgling down the overflow and mounds of bubbles topped the tub walls. Angie turned, his slowly sweeping gaze making her very much aware of her nudity. Deke looked every inch a Texan in his boots, tan cords, leather vest and hat.

"I thought I'd have time to take a bath and change before you arrived," Angie explained.

"Go ahead." Deke removed his hat and hooked it on the doorknob, running a hand through his hair to comb out the flatness. "There's no point in letting the water get cold."

"Will you keep me company?" She hesitated, then stepped into the tub and sank down amid the perfumed bubbles.

"I planned on it. I'll pull up a chair and watch," Deke assured her dryly, and he closed the lid on the toilet seat to sit down. Leaning forward, he rested his elbows on his knees and loosely linked his hands together. "How was the traffic?"

"Bad," Angie laughed ruefully and soaped the washcloth. She could feel the weight of his gaze as she spread the lather over her arms, shoulders and neck. "On top of that, the radiator hose broke and I was delayed while it was being repaired." It was a decidedly sensuous feeling to bathe while Deke watched, squeezing warm water over her skin to rinse away the soap. "How was the game?" She looked up as Deke moved from his seat to the side of the tub, unbuttoning his cuffs and rolling back the sleeves.

"Dallas won." Kneeling beside the tub, he took the washcloth and soap from her unresisting fingers. Angie couldn't think of anything more enjoyable than having Deke bathe her. He began washing her back, his hand moving in slow, circular motions over her shoulders and ribs and along her spine.

"I'll bet Lindy was thrilled to see her idols in person," she mused with her eyes closed, wanting to purr like a cat.

"What do you mean?" There was a slight hesitation in his motion, a brief tensing before it continued.

"The Dallas Cowboy cheerleaders. Lindy wants to be one when she grows up," Angie replied and tipped her head forward, enjoying his massage. "Mmmm, that feels good," she murmured.

"How do you know that?" Deke concentrated his efforts on a near shoulder.

"Marissa told me." A delicious warmth was flowing through her limbs, a combination of hot bath water and the pervading caress of his hand.

"When did you talk to her?" The soap-slick washcloth wandered across her breastbone, prompting Angie to lift her chin. Her lashes drifted open so she could look at the man she loved, his rugged face so close to hers. Her lips laid together softly, moist and shining. Deke noticed them, but he ignored their silent invitation.

Angie was tired of his cross-examination, but she was aware of his distrust and she wanted to reassure him that he had no cause for concern. "When I was in Goliad." She felt the faint tension dissipate at her answer.

Almost as a reward, Deke guided the washcloth in his hand to a breast, encasing it in lather and gently rubbing it in until the action bordered on erotic fondling. A faint sound of immense pleasure came from her throat and he duplicated the process on her other breast. Angie closed her eyes to savor the warm rapture in his touch.

"I thought you might change your mind and decide to stay in Houston," Deke murmured.

Without opening her eyes, Angie slowly shook her head from side to side. "It never even occurred to me."

"Did you see that Sullivan character while you were there?" The question was undercoated with a low-level challenge.

Without opening her eyes all the way, Angie stole a glance at him through her lashes. Could Deke be jealous? It was a lilting thought.

"Yes," she admitted. "Ted stopped by the apartment." She saw the hardness in his eyes, but his expression was otherwise bland.

"What did he have to say?" Instead of looking at her, he was studying the firm contours of her wet breasts.

"He apologized for his previous behavior. Mostly he came to say goodbye." Angie couldn't make up her mind whether Deke was jealous or simply disliked Ted.

"Does he know you're living with me?"

His bluntly worded question stole some of her pleasure. She had never applied that term to their situation. They were living together, but the phrase made it seem so immoral. It didn't feel wrong.

"Yes." Her voice was soft, a little subdued.

"Didn't he advise you against it?" Deke challenged.

"Yes," Angie admitted that, too, and remembered what Ted had said about Deke's actions. She wanted Ted to be wrong, and she knew she had to find out. "He said you were stringing me along with Lindy for bait. That you have no intention of letting me see her."

"Is that right?" Deke countered with an indifferent remark, but there was an underlying harshness in his tone, a biting impatience.

"I told him you would." She searched his face for some clue to confirm her belief, but his impassive features yielded nothing. "You will, won't you?"

"We need time." The washcloth stopped caressing her and began to scrub, echoing the roughness in his reply.

Angie caught at his wrist, checking his motion. "How long before I can see her, Deke?" If he loved her, he wouldn't keep her separated from Lindy. She had to test him.

"Don't push it, Angie," he warned, a flare of anger in his gray eyes.

But she persisted, because she had to know how he felt toward her—if he cared. "Christmas is coming. I will see her before then, won't I?" Her blue eyes were rounded in silent appeal.

The muscles along his jaw bunched as it tightened. All in one motion, Deke pulled away and rolled to his feet, towering above her. "Dammit, I said don't push it!" The washcloth was hurled into the bathwater, its resultant splash punctuating his angry statement.

Instinctively Angie recoiled from the spray. When she looked back, Deke was striding from the room, grabbing his hat off the doorknob as he went by. For a second, she was too stunned to move.

"Deke!" But even as she called him, Angie knew he wouldn't come back. Even if it showed a shameless lack of pride, she didn't want him to leave, not as long as there was a breath of a chance for them.

Stepping hurriedly out of the slippery tub, she pulled the thick bath towel off the rack and made a haphazard attempt to dry the water dripping from her. Then she was running after him, wrapping the towel around her as she went.

"Deke!" Her heart pounded in her throat until it ached. Angie raced down the hallway through the living room to the door standing open at the top of the stairs. "Deke!" But he wasn't in sight. She stopped, realizing she hadn't been quick enough to catch him. Tears burned the back of her eyes as she turned away from the stairs.

A brief movement in the living room caught her eye. Deke was standing by the drink cabinet with a glass in his hand. For a second Angie thought he was a figment of her imagination, but the hard feel of his eyes was real. She crossed the space between them in a wild daze.

"I thought you'd gone," Angie murmured.

"I should have." Deke bolted down the drink as if to put out a fire raging inside of him, then studied the bottom of the empty glass with grim absorption.

She lowered her gaze to his shirt front. "I'm glad you didn't." Her voice wavered with relief.

The glass was set aside. "Are you?" His hands moved to the towel where it was tucked around her. Deke loosened it and let it fall to the floor. Then he placed his hands high on her ribcage and covered the button-points of her breasts with his thumbs. "Why don't you show me how glad you are?" he challenged huskily.

Angie couldn't breathe. She was dimly aware of the sun's setting rays streaming in through the windows which meant the drapes were open. Anyone could see in.

"Deke, the windows . . . the neighbors . . ." She was too rawly aware of awakened desire to put the words together in a sentence.

"To hell with the neighbors," he muttered, but he picked her up and carried her out of the living room away from any peeping eyes. He set her down in the middle of the bedroom. "I'm always undressing you," Deke stated. "This time you're going to undress me."

Her fingers trembled at the new experience as she reached to unfasten his shirt buttons.

Chapter Ten

Something fresh and sparkling entered their relationship. Angie wasn't sure whether love had given her a new outlook or they had reached a higher plateau. Deke seemed less reserved. His lazy smile appeared more often and sometimes his eyes gleamed with possessive gentleness. Yet Lindy remained a forbidden topic, and Angie was too insecure to broach it and risk losing what little she had.

Two days into December, a weather front moved in. A cold wind moaned outside the kitchen windows while Angie fixed breakfast for the two of them. In Texas vernacular, it was known as a "blue norther" that swept down from the northern plains. They usually accused the "snowbirds" coming south for the winter of leaving the gate open and letting the cold weather through.

"Do you want to go to the beach this morning?" Deke asked when Angie set their plates of pancakes and sausage on the counter.

The invitation took her by surprise. They'd never done anything together in the daytime. Deke had always left right after breakfast, and she didn't see him again until night. She was thrown by this proposed change in their routine. There was confusion in her look.

"Don't you have to leave?" She watched him casually spreading butter between his pancakes.

There was a vague lift of his shoulders. "Not necessarily." He poured maple syrup over the stack and passed the syrup pitcher to Angie. "The boys can handle things at the ranch for one morning." It was a weekday, Angie realized, so Lindy would be at school. "If you don't want to go, that's all right."

"I do." She didn't want him to doubt that.

His glance roamed over her in warm approval before he shifted his attention to the food. "You'll have to dress warm. It'll be blustery on the island."

"I will."

Her hooded windbreaker was lined for warmth. Under it, Angie wore a turtleneck sweater of black wool, while the heavy fabric of her light blue corduroys offered protection for her legs. With thick socks and rubber-soled walking shoes, she was ready to combat the elements.

Deke looked equally prepared in his own way as he sat behind the wheel of the car. His hat was pushed low and straight on his head. The western cut of his corduroy jacket was lined with sheepskin, leather patches on the sleeves at the elbows, and the collar was turned up in expectation of the wind. Dark blue Levis and boots completed his outfit.

The ferry chugged its way across the channel to its slip on Mustang Island, carrying only a handful of cars on its short journey, to the resort town of Port Aransas. Gray clouds rolled and tumbled in the skies overhead, blown by the strong north wind. A few seagulls struggled against it, pushed to a standstill before surrendering and soaring away on its currents. On previous trips to the island seven years ago, Angie remembered porpoises looping through the water alongside the ferry to usher it across the channel. She spied none in the waters today. They'd be back, when the front had blown through and the Texas winter sun returned.

As the ferry nosed into its slip, there was a brief scurry of activity to make it fast. Deke started the car's engine in preparation to disembark. A few minutes later, they were rolling off. Mustang Island was a barrier island, one of a string that protects the Gulf coastline of Texas. They turned on the road leading to the long stretch of sandy beach on the Gulf side of the island.

It was practically deserted except for a few hardy souls. The fair-weather fishermen were not to be seen, and shell-collectors were waiting for a warmer day to venture on the sands. They drove on the firmly packed sand, a foaming gray-green surf sending curling waves crashing into shore on one side and creamy sand dunes with tall stands of sea oats rising in mounds on the other. Past the fishing piers, the cabanas and bathhouses, Deke found an empty stretch of beach and parked the car.

His glance slid to Angie. "Want to walk awhile?"

"Sure." She climbed out on the passenger side and walked around the car to join him.

The wind nipped at her face. Deke waited while she put her hood up and tied the string under her chin, then he took her hand to walk along the beach. The heavy surf drowned out all other sound as it pounded the sand. With the turbulent sea, the rolling gray clouds, and the blustery wind, there was something raw and wild about the morning—and they had it all to themselves.

They stayed close to the tidewater mark out of the reach of the waves. Driftwood—pieces of lumber and trees—were scattered on the shore, stringy with seaweed and barnacles. Pieces of brittle sand dollars, angel-wings and shark-eyes dotted the sand, along with other mollusk shells. The sea was giving up its treasures, surrendering them at the feet of the island.

The weathered trunk of a long-dead tree lay

high on the beach, the charred remnants of some camper's fire in front of it. The elements had smoothed the trunk's surface, turning it into a natural bench. Deke led her to it.

"Let's sit down," he suggested.

With their backs to the wind, they sat on the log and faced the rolling Gulf seas. Deke put his arm around her and gathered her against the shelter of his chest and shoulder, locking his hands around her middle. Angie rested her head against him.

"Remember when you found that rock with the fossilized remains of a scorpion out here in the dunes," she recalled. "I wonder how it got here?"

"It's hard to say." Deke didn't venture a guess.

"I suppose," she murmured absently.

"Angie." His voice was low, distantly contemplative. "Why didn't you come to me when you found out you were pregnant that summer? Why did your aunt and my parents know about it before I did?"

He was breaking all the rules by bringing up the past. Angie floundered in the sudden turnabout. "I wasn't sure I was pregnant. When I started getting sick in the mornings, my aunt got suspicious and hustled me off to a doctor. She called your parents before I had a chance to tell you. Then all three of you came over." It wasn't a pleasant memory.

"I remember." Deke sounded grim. "All the while they were discussing you and your 'condition,' you wouldn't even look at me. Why?"

She recalled the stark embarrassment of that afternoon. The burning heat of it swept over her again and she moved out of his arms to stand and let the norther wrap its cool wind around her. Angie heard the crunch of sand under his boots and knew he was behind her.

"I was ashamed," she finally answered his question. "They were talking about us. And they knew you and I had—" Even now she couldn't say it.

"—that you and I had made love." Deke filled in the blank for her. "Were you ashamed that they knew?"

"Yes, I was ashamed." Angie lowered her head. "I was seventeen. I'd always been taught only bad girls did things like that." She blinked at the tears stinging her eyes. "I was confused and frightened. And you seemed so angry that day." Angie thought back to his first question and turned around to face him. "Were you angry because I hadn't told you first?"

"Probably." He was studying her with a faintly narrowed look, his hands shoved into his jacket pockets. "What did you think had made me angry?"

"I thought you were mad because I was pregnant—because you had to marry me." Angie looked away and tucked a strand of hair inside the hood that the wind had whipped free.

"I said I was willing to marry you," Deke reminded her.

"I know what you said," Angie countered.

"But you also told me the day we were married that you wouldn't have done it if I hadn't been pregnant."

"Not then." He pulled his hands out of his pockets to grip her shoulders. "You were too young. I would rather have waited until you were older. I should never had laid my hands on you in the first place, but once I did, I couldn't keep them off you, so you got pregnant." His features darkened with intensity as his gaze pierced her. "Did you ever love me, Angie?" There was a desperate anger in him to know the answer.

"Deke, I did." She moved into his arms, sliding her hands around his middle and pressing her cheek against the rough corduroy of his jacket. "I do," she whispered against the cloth, but it muffled her words.

His hand crooked under her chin and lifted it. When his mouth descended onto hers, his hard masculine lips were cool against hers, but they gradually became a source of heat that burned through her. It welded them together for a long moment, erasing some of the scars from old wounds that had not completely healed until now.

When they drew apart, Angie curved her hand to his jaw, reveling in its strength. Deke captured her hand and pressed his mouth to her fingers, then he e closed it between both of his hands.

"Your hands are cold," he murmured with a warm glitter in his look.

"So are yours," Angie countered softly.

186

"Maybe we'd better walk back to the car," he suggested and wrapped an arm around her shoulders, pointing her back the way they'd come.

Distance made the car seem small. Angie hadn't realized they'd walked so far. They didn't hurry.

The sun was warm on her back as Angie leaned into the car to reach the packages in the back seat. The "blue norther" had moved out of the area several days ago, replaced by summerlike weather. With her arms and hands full of packages, Angie closed the car door with a push of her hip.

"Beautiful day, isn't it?" A neighbor remarked.

Angie looked up and smiled an agreement at the elderly woman puttering in the flowerbed next door. "It certainly is."

"I see you've been doing some Christmas shopping." The woman's sharp eyes had spotted the corner of a holiday-wrapped box sticking out of a sack. "Did you go to Corpus?" she asked with friendly curiosity, shortening the name of the closest large city, Corpus Christi.

"Yes." She had gone on somewhat of a shopping spree, buying Christmas gifts for Deke, Lindy and Marissa. Angie was getting excited about Christmas for the first time in quite awhile. "I'd better get these in the house." She had spoken to the woman several times in the past week, but it was usually just a casual greeting and an odd comment about the weather. She didn't expect any differently this time.

"Excuse me," the woman called her back when Angie would have started to the door. "I've been trying to remember where I'd seen you before. Aren't you Lillie Franklin's niece?"

"Yes, she was my aunt," Angie admitted.

"You spent the summer with her a few years back," the woman recalled clearly now. "You and Deke Blackwood were quite thick then, weren't you?"

"Yes." She felt self-conscious, aware that the neighbor had to have noticed Deke's nightly coming and going.

"I remember at the time, Lillie was worried that the two of you were getting too serious, but I reminded her how intense summer romances always seemed." A reminiscent smile touched her mouth. "As it turns out, I was partially right. It wasn't too long after you left that young Blackwood got married. Of course, his poor wife died giving birth to their child."

"So I heard," Angie murmured uncomfortably.

The woman was too caught up in her recollections of the past to notice Angie's unease. "Her death was quite a shock to him. For several summers, he was brooding and withdrawn. Every time Harold and I saw him, he was alone." A thoughtful frown creased her forehead. "Sometimes when you see a person out walking, you don't think anything about it.

They're just walking somewhere. You don't think of them as being sad or lonely. But there was a quality about young Blackwood. You sensed he had lost some vital part of his life. I guess there are two kinds of alone," she concluded.

"Perhaps there are," Angie agreed.

A knowing twinkle brightened the woman's gaze as she eyed Angie curiously. "It seems that you've managed to rekindle that old romance since you've returned. Young Blackwood is here frequently. I hope you're able to help him get over his late wife."

"I hope so, too." What an impossible situation. How could she explain to the woman that she and Deke's supposedly dead wife were the same person?

"Are you just visiting or will you be staying for awhile?" the elderly neighbor asked inquisitively.

"It hasn't been decided." Angie sought an excuse to break away from this conversation. "I'd love to stay and chat, but I really have to go."

"It's nearly dinner time, isn't it?" the woman realized. "Come over for coffee some morning."

"Thanks." Angie hurried toward the front door before anything more was said.

When Deke arrived that evening, Angie was setting the table. She gave him a smile as he entered the dining room and continued laying out the silverware settings.

"What's this?" He picked up one of the Christmas presents from the stack on the bureau where a nativity scene was displayed. "Have you been shopping?"

"Yes, I went into Corpus Christi today," she replied absently.

"You didn't mention anything about going this morning," Deke frowned, lifting a curious eyebrow.

"It was too nice a day to stay home," she explained the impulse.

"What time did you get back?" He wandered over to the table, stopping on the opposite side from her.

"I'm not sure. Around four, I think. The lady next door was working in her yard when I drove in. I talked to her for awhile before I came in. It was after four then," Angie told him.

"Mrs. Osborne?"

"She didn't tell me her name." She smoothed her hands over her skirt, suddenly nervous about the question she was going to ask. "Deke, why did you tell everybody that your wife died?"

His glance flicked over her, becoming remote. "I believe I said Lindy's mother died."

"It's the same thing," Angie countered with sudden impatience.

"I chose to differentiate," he stated.

"Why? It's me. I'm one in the same person." It was difficult for her to accept that Deke had cut her out of his life that way. "Why did you have to say I was dead?"

"Because I didn't want my daughter to know that her mother hadn't wanted her!" he flared. "Lindy had done nothing to deserve that kind of cold-hearted rejection except to be born, so I saw no reason for her to suffer from it."

"It wasn't cold-hearted," Angie protested.

"How was Lindy to know that? How can a mere child understand why the mother who is supposed to love her doesn't even want to be a part of her life?" His hands gripped the straight back of a chair, all his muscles showing the tension of anger.

"But I did love her—and I do love her," she insisted. "Can't you see that?"

"That's what you say." He showed his skepticism.

"I came back," Angie reminded him. "Doesn't it prove anything to you that I'm here?"

"But for how long?" Deke was practically shouting.

"What do I have to do to get through to you that I'm sincere?" she cried helplessly. "I've already given up my career, my home, everything I've worked for all these years. Now the whole neighborhood—probably the whole town—knows that I'm living here as your mistress. So I've even sacrificed my pride and self-respect. What more do you want me to give up?"

"Yourself!" He swung away as if unable to contain all that raging energy any longer and went striding out of the room.

White with shock, Angie watched him disappear and winced when she heard the stair door violently slammed shut. A minute later she heard the revving motor of his car and the squeal of tires as it shot out of the drive.

The evening meal she had prepared was never eaten. In bed, Angie tossed and turned, unable to sleep. Flashbacks of other conversations kept running through her mind. They were dominated by Ted's warning that Deke was just using her, dangling the promise of Lindy in front of her, but always out of reach. She didn't want to believe it of him, but it was becoming blatantly obvious by his actions.

The next morning, Angie didn't bother with breakfast. She dressed, got in her car and drove straight to the elementary school Lindy attended. Bells rang for morning recess as she entered the building. When she neared the second-grade classroom, her gaze scanned the children filing out. Lindy's teacher, Mrs. Gonzales, brought up the rear.

"Mrs. Gonzales!" Angie hurried to catch up to the young teacher who paused at the sound of her name. "I'm not sure if you remember me," she began.

"Yes, you were here about a month ago," the brunette smiled. "I thought you were on your vacation."

"I was," Angie admitted but didn't explain. "I came to see Lindy Blackwood."

"She isn't here," the teacher shook her head

and tried not to show her curiosity for Angie's sake.

"You mean, she's not in school today?" Angie frowned, because it didn't make sense that Deke would still be keeping her home.

"No, I meant she doesn't go to school here anymore," Mrs. Gonzales clarified her answer. "I'm really not too surprised. Deke Blackwood can certainly afford to send his daughter to a private school. It's odd that he transferred her in mid-term though."

"A private school." Angie felt her heart sinking. "Do you know which one?"

"No, I'm afraid I don't." The teacher grimaced apologetically.

"Is there any way I could find out?"

The brunette was puzzled by the urgent tone in Angie's voice. "You could check at the principal's office. They might know," she suggested without promising anything.

"Thank you." Angie hurried away.

The same plump receptionist was on duty. She greeted Angie with a friendly smile when she entered the principal's office.

"May I help you?" she asked.

"Yes. I'd like some information about a second-grade student who was enrolled here— a Miss Lindy Blackwood." Angie tried to sound very businesslike. "Would you check your records and tell me what school she is attending now?"

"I'm sorry." The receptionist didn't even bother to look. "I'm afraid we don't have that information. You see, Mr. Blackwood obtained a transcript of his daughter's school record when he signed her out, so it wouldn't be necessary for her new school to contact us."

Angie started to leave, then thought of another question. "Can you tell me approximately how long ago she changed schools?"

"It's been more than a month ago, I'm sure," the receptionist answered.

"I see," Angie murmured and turned away.

Leaving the school lot, she drove back to the house on the Key. She wasn't willing to give up her search yet. She went straight to the phone in the kitchen and opened the telephone directory to the list of private schools in the area. She called every one, but none had a student registered under the name of Lindy Blackwood, and all claimed no child had transferred to their school in the recent past.

Faced with another dead end, Angie slid onto a counter stool and chewed on a fingernail. It was possible Deke had sent Lindy to a boarding school some distance away. But where? And how could she find out? There was one person who could tell her. Marissa had proved to be her ally once. She might be again? Angie reached for the phone and dialed the number. If Deke answered, she could pretend she had been calling him.

"This is the Blackwood Ranch." The phone was answered by a woman, but Angie didn't recognize her voice.

"Who am I speaking to?" she asked.

"This is Jessie. I'm the housekeeper," the woman identified herself.

"May I talk to Marissa, please?"

"I'm sorry. She isn't here."

"Oh. When will she be back?"

"I don't know, ma'm," the housekeeper replied.

"She'll be there this evening, won't she?" Angie inquired.

"No. She isn't living here right now," the woman explained.

Stunned, Angie raked her fingers through her hair, combing it severely away from her face. She couldn't believe Deke could be so callous as to turn Marissa out of her own home. Then she realized Marissa had to be with Lindy. Deke hadn't sent her away to boarding school at such a young age.

"Can you tell me how I can get in touch with Marissa?" Angie asked. "Do you have an address or a phone number where she can be reached?"

"I don't, but Deke could give it to you," the housekeeper replied.

Angie held her breath, suddenly wary. "Is he there?"

"Not right now, but he will be a little later. Shall I have him call you?" the woman suggested helpfully.

"No, that's all right." Angie shook her head in slight relief. "I'll probably talk to him later this evening. Thank you."

A cold hand closed around her heart and squeezed it as she hung up the phone. She felt betrayed by Deke. He'd led her to believe that Lindy was still here, that she was still at the ranch. And all the time he'd sent her away. And Marissa had gone with her.

There wasn't any way Marissa could have let her know. Deke had seen to that, too. Angie was certain that Marissa had no idea she was living in their summer house. She wouldn't know how to contact her. Even Ted had told her that when he called the motel in Goliad, they had informed him she'd left without a forwarding address.

How many times had Deke congratulated himself for being so clever. She shut her eyes when she thought of all the times he must have been secretly laughing at her for being so naive. And she had never guessed. She had been so in love with him that she never once suspected.

Why had he done this to her? Did he hate her that much? How could she still love him? But there wasn't any rhyme or reason to its existence.

Angie was lost, cut adrift with nothing to cling to and nowhere to go. Deke had probably planned on that, too. She hadn't realized he could be so ruthless. Ted had seen it, but she had been blinded by her love.

Chapter Eleven

 $\mathscr{C}$ urled in a tight ball in a chair with her arms hugged about her knees, Angie heard a vehicle pull into the drive. It sounded like a truck. She tensed, a rawness licking through her nerves, at the slam of a door. It wasn't five o'clock yet, still she knew it was Deke, even though it hadn't been his car.

Her wary gaze centered on the door. There were footsteps on the stairs, taking them two at a time. Angie hadn't seen Deke since he'd stormed out of the house the night before. She steeled herself for this meeting.

When he reached the top of the stairs and saw her, there was the slightest hesitation in his stride before Deke entered the living room. There was a tired, dusty look about him from his faded, work-stained Levis and the run-down heels of his boots to the dried perspiration marks of his chambray shirt. Usually he showered and changed into clean clothes before coming to see her, but this time he'd come straight off the ranch. He carried the markings of a long day, yet it gave him a rough vigor. His hard, sinewy frame was resilient, imbued with a potency that quickened her pulse.

Deke took off his dusty hat and dropped it on an empty chair seat. "You called the ranch today." It was a statement that had no hint of doubt as she came under the attention of his steel gray eyes.

What did he think she was going to do? Deny it and lie? Or meekly apologize? Although her behavior might have given him the impression she was submissive, Angie knew that wasn't her nature. And she wasn't going to sit there while he towered over her like some all-righteous god either.

Unclasping her hands, she swung her legs to the floor and stood up. She tucked her trembling fingers inside the hip pockets of her white jeans and adopted a pose of nonchalance as she wandered out of his range of domination.

"Yes, I called the ranch," Angie admitted in a voice that was tight but otherwise steady. "I wanted to talk to Marissa."

"You went to the school today, too." Again his flat statement was a positive accusation.

Angie didn't bother to ask how he knew that. He had probably gotten suspicious after the housekeeper had told him about the phone call and checked with the principal's office. After that, it had been a simple matter of adding two and two.

"Yes," she admitted that, too, and turned to level her own accusation at him. "They told me Lindy had been transferred to another school."

His mouth thinned into a cold line. "I wondered how long it would be before you went behind my back."

"Is that your justification for lying to me?" Angie didn't try to contain her hurt anger. She let it flame and sent it out to burn him. "Two wrongs don't make a right, Deke! I didn't go behind your back! I just didn't wait for your permission to see my daughter! I don't give a damn what any words say on a piece of paper! You don't have any God-given right to keep me away from my daughter!"

"Don't preach to me about rights!" Deke snapped. "You gave up yours seven years ago!"

"And you're never going to forget that, are you?" she realized. "Where is she? Where have you taken Lindy?"

"Do you really think I'll tell you?" he taunted and raked her with a look.

Everything male about him challenged her. Angie wanted to lash out at him—to strike him and inflict some of the pain on him. But his superior physical strength would have negated any assault by her. Angie stifled that urge with a trembling effort.

"How long, Deke?" she demanded. "I want to know how long you've been lying to me? When did you send Lindy away with Marissa?"

Deke seemed to consider his answer before he spoke. "They left the day you moved in here." He watched the information wash the color from her face. Even though it confirmed the half-formed suspicion she'd had, Angie still reeled from the extent of his deception.

"And you brought me here not so I could be close to Lindy, but so Marissa wouldn't know where to find me," she guessed.

There was a complacent lift to the corners of his mouth. "Why do you think my sister called you at the motel that morning?"

Angie made another guess and watched his taunting smile deepen at her accuracy. "She was going to warn me about what you were planning."

"But I intercepted the message before it could be delivered."

Angie remembered how he had commandeered the phone that morning, so smoothly without hesitation. "You guessed that she might call me, didn't you?" she accused, a bitter taste on her tongue.

"It was possible," Deke acknowledged it hadn't been unexpected.

"Is that why you stayed all night with me,

200

Deke?" Angie felt sick. Nothing was turning out to be the way it seemed at the time.

"You know damn well it wasn't the only reason I stayed." Deke was impatient with her. "There were a half dozen ways I could have prevented Marissa from contacting you that didn't entail spending the night."

"But none quite so convenient." She was sweetly sarcastic to him.

"Maybe not, but it was merely a side benefit!" Deke snapped.

It was all becoming very sordid and painful. She had been used, that much was plain. There would be time to cry over that later. Now, Angie needed to know where she stood with regard to Lindy. She wasn't going to accept any more indefinite replies.

"Let's stop all this pretense, Deke," Angie demanded. "You got me here by hinting that you would eventually allow me to see Lindy. I don't want to hear any more of your lies and half-truths. Just give it to me straight for a change."

Deke reacted aggressively to the challenge, bristling like a male animal. "You want to know where you stand, do you? You are in the same position you've always been in. You don't have a chance of seeing Lindy without my say-so! You don't know where she is. You don't even know where to look. And you'll never find her unless I tell you."

"That's kidnapping! I'll take you to court!" Angie threatened.

"You take me to court!" he dared her. "I'll keep that case so tied up with postponements and appeals, Lindy will be eighteen before a final verdict is ever issued!"

Fighting him was hopeless. Angie knew it and hot tears burned her eyes. "You're a heartless bastard," she hissed in frustration. "Now I know why I didn't stay married to you!"

She had the satisfaction of seeing his features darken with anger. Before Angie could stalk out of the room with the last word issued by her, Deke caught her arm and roughly yanked her back. She strained against his grip, intimidated by the silver blaze in his eyes.

"If you leave this house, Angie, I swear by all that's holy you'll never see Lindy again!" Deke threatened.

"Why are you keeping me here?" she stormed in confusion. "You despise me! You can't possibly be that desperate for a mistress!"

"Not anyone will do," he denied that and caught her other arm when she tried to break away. His strong fingers curled into the tender flesh of her upper arms as he hauled her struggling body closer. "You're the one who satisfies me. You're here because I want you."

"No!" She struggled wildly, hating him as passionately as she loved him, twisting and kicking, but she couldn't escape.

His powerfully muscled arms crushed her to his length, bending her back to put her off balance. Her hands pushed ineffectively at the looming wall of his chest. Tucking her chin in, Angie tried to keep her head down, but Deke was having none of that. His large hand captured the underside of her jaw and forced her head back until she thought her neck would snap.

There was no eluding him. His mouth came down to ravage her lips plundering their softness and smothering her animal cries of protest. She was held so tightly she could hardly breathe. Each second the brutal kiss continued, it drained more of her strength. Blackness swam on the fringes of her conscious mind.

When her body stopped straining from him in stiff resistance, Deke dragged his mouth from hers and let go of her throat, placing that hand on her hip to keep her within his arms. Angie was trembling, drinking in air while her bruised lips throbbed from his roughness. Her hands remained braced against his chest in a weak attempt to keep him at a distance until she had gathered some of her strength back.

Deke took advantage of her temporary passivity. The hand on her hip made a single, smooth stroke up her waist to her breast. His hand remained there in bold possession as Angie flashed him a smouldering look.

"If there was an ounce of honesty in your body," Deke challenged, "you'd admit that you're here because you want me, too."

"No," she denied it quickly, too quickly.

"Yes," he insisted with a dangerous gleam in his eyes. "Your heart is racing and your nipple is hard in my hand."

"No." She tried desperately to deny his claim, but her treacherous senses told her it was true. Angie realized that she would have fought till her last breath at any attempt to overpower her physically, but she was vulnerable to seduction, especially Deke's brand. And he knew that the response he hadn't obtained with sheer force could be gotten with a sensual caress.

"Yes, Angie, yes." His arms encircled her.

When she turned her head aside to avoid his kiss, Deke raised no objections, seeking instead the sensitive curve of her neck and the evocative hollow below her ear. His roaming hands explored her body and followed the curve of her spine. He knew every place that aroused her pleasure, and he exploited that knowledge to the fullest.

Sensation buffeted her at every turn. The male scent of him enveloped her while the blood pounded in her ears. Her flesh was tingling from its contact with the unyielding contours of his body and the stimulating caress of his hands. His mouth grazed its way across her cheek and teased the corners of her lips until she turned her head to taste the warmth of his kiss. And she was lost.

The minute she was pliant in his hands, Deke lifted his head a scant inch, letting the heat of his breath fan her lips. "You want me, don't you?" he murmured thickly, demanding her full capitulation. "Admit it."

A little frown of dismay swept her expression as Angie closed her eyes, hating him for forcing the admission from her. "Yes, yes, yes," she whispered in the frustration of guilt.

A second later she was swept away by his embrace, kissed deeply and passionately until she didn't care anymore. Nothing mattered as long as he touched her and held her and loved her. Deke was doing all those things and more. She felt strangely weightless. In somewhat of a daze, Angie realized Deke was carrying her.

She had barely made that discovery when he was laying her on the bed. Numbed by a heady desire, she watched him stand by the bed and unbutton his shirt to strip it off. Suddenly it hit her that she was falling into the same trap again. Nothing had been resolved by their argument. Letting him make love to her after trying to take a stand would only compound the problem.

"No!" Angie came to her senses.

As she rolled toward the opposite side of the bed, she felt the mattress dip under his weight. Then he was catching her and trying to drag her back. She fought to escape, hitting and kicking, but she was no match for him.

"Stop it, Angie." He pinned her arms to the mattress while his body held hers down. She halted her struggles briefly to look at him, breathing hard. "You aren't fighting me,"

Deke told her. "You're fighting yourself. It's no good, Angie. You can't win that fight."

He was right. She knew it and a limpness went through her body. She wanted him. She had always wanted him. She loved him. It was all so hopeless. Angie began to cry with tearless, silent sobs.

"I've fought the battle myself," Deke murmured and gently smoothed the hair away from her neck. "It's something neither one of us can control."

"That's not a good enough reason," she protested softly, because she needed his love, not just his lust.

"Yes, it is." And he kissed her slowly to prove it. Then his proof went beyond kisses to a union of the flesh that transcended mere desire. The completeness of it left Angie pleasurably exhausted and somehow reassured. Or maybe the reassurance came from the arms that stayed around her and held her close.

When Angie awakened the next morning, Deke wasn't in bed. She glanced sharply toward the bathroom, but there were no sounds to indicate his presence. Then she noticed the note propped against the lamp on the bedside table. She rolled over to reach it and had to pause when a wave of dizzyness drained her.

Fighting the lightheaded feeling, she sat up carefully on the edge of the bed and waited until it receded. It frightened her briefly until she remembered that she hadn't eaten at all yesterday. Lack of food would certainly make her weak and dizzy. Angie reached for the note and unfolded to read its message.

Angie,
   You were sleeping so peacefully I didn't have the heart to wake you. I just wanted you to know that I'll be out of town for a couple of days. I expect to be back Thursday.

                              Deke

Not a single word that was remotely personal or affectionate. She wanted to cry, although she supposed it was considerate of him to forewarn her of his absence so she wouldn't be worrying or wondering where he was. But that was cold comfort. She started to get up and had to sit down as another wave of nausea washed through her. She simply had to get some food in her stomach.

By early afternoon, Angie felt fine. She did a little cleaning, washed some clothes and fixed herself a light supper. She went to bed early and slept the night through. But when she woke up Wednesday morning, the nausea was back. The little fear that had been gnawing at the back of her mind insisted on being faced. She was pregnant.

Angie's first impulse was to pack and run, but what would running solve? There was still the issue of Lindy to be settled. Although she dreaded telling Deke, he had a right to know. There was always the chance she wasn't pregnant. It might just be a false alarm, a touch of the flu or some food that didn't agree with her. There was only one way to confirm it.

Angie called the Physicians Bureau and had them recommend an obstetrician. Then she phoned his office and made an appointment for Friday. The dilemma remained whether to tell Deke when he came back on Thursday or wait until she had the tests back from the doctor.

It was a decision she hadn't made when Deke arrived at the house Thursday night. She had dinner ready so there was little need for conversation. He told her about his trip to Kingsville to buy some registered cattle. After they'd finished the meal, he went into the living room while she cleared the table. She joined him in a few minutes, leaving the dishes to wash the next day.

"You're awfully quiet tonight," Deke observed, and he studied her much too closely.

"Am I?" Angie tried to smile but she knew the attempt at brightness hadn't succeeded.

"It's still Lindy, isn't it?" he decided with a grimness tightening his jaw.

Angie moved to the large windows and looked out in an effort to avoid a discussion. She heard Deke come up behind her and she turned before he could touch her. He eyed her with an uncertain look, trying to discover why she was being so elusive. His inspecting gaze picked out the slight pallor in her complexion.

"Are you feeling all right?" he asked.

"N . . . Not really, no," she admitted, coming to a decision at last. There was a faintly defiant tilt of her chin. "I think I'm pregnant."

Her announcement rippled through him, bringing a frown to his expression as his narrowed gaze swept over her slim figure. "Are you sure?"

"I have an appointment tomorrow at the doctor's. I won't know for certain until the results come back from the tests." Her body had already told her it was merely a formality. "But I'm sure."

Angie watched his features harden in what appeared to be a surge of anger and something shriveled up inside of her. She had hoped . . . If he could have been happy about it . . . A terrible, wrenching ache tore at her heart as Deke turned away from her toward the window.

"Damn!" The flat of his hand struck the window frame with a shuddering force and Angie jerked her head to the side at the sound.

"I thought you should know—" Her voice was hoarse with the strain of attempting normal speech. "—before I left."

"Leave?" Deke pivoted to face her. "You're not going anywhere. We can be married—"

"No!" Angie violently rejected his suggestion. "I wouldn't marry you if you were the last man on earth, Deke Blackwood!"

He drew back as if she'd struck him. And Angie knew she couldn't spend another minute in his house. She had to leave before Deke managed to persuade her they could make it work. This was no different than the last time. There was never a marriage without love.

With tears filling her eyes, she started for the door, walking faster with each step until she was running. She heard Deke coming after her, which only panicked her.

"Dammit, Angie!" His angry voice broke over her. "You're not going anywhere! You're staying right here!"

She had reached the stairs when he grabbed her arm to stop her. Angie whirled around so violently that he lost his hold. Her foot slipped off the top step and she started to fall. She grabbed for the railing to try to save herself, but her fingers couldn't grasp it. In the next second, she was falling helplessly. She screamed Deke's name. Then there was pain, shooting colors blinding her eyes and then blackness.

"Angie!" Deke chased her tumbling body down the stairs, not catching up with her until she came to a stop more than halfway to the bottom. It was all a nightmare to him. White-faced and sweating, Deke knelt down next to her unconscious form. There was a gash on her forehead oozing blood. His first impulse was to gather her up in his arms, but caution warned him not to move her. "My God, Angie," he groaned. "What have I done to you?"

He pressed his trembling fingers against her neck and felt life pulsing beneath his touch. Relief shook him. He had never known such heart-stopping fear or such an agonizing feeling of helplessness as he had when he'd watched her falling and been unable to reach her.

"Thank God, she's alive," Deke murmured, clenching his hands into impotent fists.

It was an effort to make his legs stop shaking and carry him up the steps to the phone. He dialed the emergency number for the ambulance and rushed back to her side as soon as he was assured they were on their way. Not once did she move during all the agonizing minutes of waiting for the ambulance to arrive. Deke stared at her deathly pale face and knew a greater hell than any he'd gone through before.

Deke rode in the ambulance with Angie, holding her limp hand to reassure himself. His eyes never let their gaze stray from her face, clinging to her as if she was his lifeline. When they wheeled her into the emergency entrance of the hospital, Deke walked beside the stretcher.

In the emergency room, he stayed by her side, barely noticing the nurse checking the vital signs. He dragged his gaze from Angie only when the doctor walked in.

"What happened?" The attending doctor bent over his patient, making his own examination.

"She fell down a flight of stairs," Deke

replied in a voice that didn't sound like it belonged to him.

"Mmm," the doctor grunted noncommittally.

"She's pregnant," Deke said, and felt the doctor's glance.

"We'll see what we can do for both of them then," he said.

Despite his strenuous objections, Deke was banished to the waiting room. The minutes dragged while he waited for some word— any word on Angie's condition. He was alternately angry with himself for driving her to the point of running from him, impatient with the seeming slowness of the hospital staff and frightened that she might die.

He was seated in one of the vinyl-covered chairs, leaning forward with his elbows resting on his knees and his hands clasped together in a fisted prayer. The strain showed in the underlying whiteness of his tanned features as he hung his head.

When the doctor appeared, Deke looked up and sharply scanned the man's face for some advance knowledge. "Angie. How is she? Will she be all right?"

"She has a rather severe concussion, two cracked ribs, and a colorful assortment of bruises, but there is nothing to indicate any lasting damage," the doctor paused in his assessment of her injuries.

"Thank God." Deke closed his eyes tightly, the muscles along his jaw working convulsively. He let out a long breath and looked at the doctor. "Can I see her now?"

"Yes." There was another hesitation. "Mr. Blackwood, I'm afraid she lost the baby."

A twisting pain knifed him as Deke turned his head away. The doctor received the slightest of nods in a silent acknowledgment of the information. There was no other outward indication in Deke's expression to show his reaction.

Pushing to his feet, he looked at the doctor. "Where is she?"

"The nurse will take you to her room."

Deke stiffly followed the uniformed woman to a hospital room. He walked to the bed where Angie lay so quietly and stared at the intravenous tube in her arm. There was a bandage around her head, covering the cut on her forehead. Her honey-blond hair seemed dark against the pillow, its sterile whiteness almost matching the paleness of her features.

A chair was sitting by the window. Deke carried it over by the bed. The nurse glanced at him with detached sympathy when he sat down.

"Why don't you come back in the morning, Mr. Blackwood?" she suggested quietly.

There was a brief shake of his head in refusal, his gaze not leaving Angie. "I'm staying."

"There's really no point," the nurse began, then realized he wasn't going to listen to her. "Very well." She let the door swing shut as she left the room.

Deke leaned closer to the bed and gently slipped his hand under hers. His fingers slowly tightened as he closed his eyes. No sound came from him. No tears spilled from his eyes. Yet sobs of pain shook his shoulders in the grief of guilt and remorse.

Chapter Twelve

Slouched in the chair, Deke was half asleep when he heard the soft swish of the hospital room door opening. He came awake and started to sit up, then winced at the crick in his neck. He lifted his hand to massage away the muscle spasm and glanced at the door, expecting to see the nurse, or the doctor, on his morning rounds. A frown knitted his brow.

"Marissa, what are you doing here?" he demanded. "You're supposed to be in Dallas. And where's Lindy?"

"She's at the ranch with Jessie," his sister explained with gentle patience. Her glance darted to the sleeping patient in the bed. "How is she?"

"They say she's all right." But he didn't sound convinced. His muscles protested when he insisted on standing. Deke rubbed his forehead, a little groggy from a lack of sleep. "When did you get here and why are you here?"

Privately, Marissa thought if her brother had looked in the mirror lately, he would know the answers to his questions. He hadn't shaved in two days, his clothes were wrinkled, and he looked like he was out on his feet. Which he should have been by all the reports she'd gotten from the nurses. Except for catnaps in the chair, he hadn't slept in more than forty-eight hours.

"When I called the ranch yesterday, Jessie told me you were here at the hospital with Angie. Lindy and I caught a plane for Corpus Christi and arrived late last night," she told him.

"It wasn't necessary," he protested grumpily.

"Wasn't it?" Marissa chided. "You're the one who looks like death warmed over. If Angie woke up now, you'd scare her."

He rubbed the stubble on his cheek and jaw. It made a rasping sound against his hand. "I guess I need a shave."

"I guess you do," she agreed on a mocking note. "And a shower and a change of clothes wouldn't hurt either."

His gaze was pulled back to the bed. "Later."

"Deke, it isn't going to do Angie any good to see you like this," she murmured, but he didn't pay attention to her. "Deke, they told me she lost the baby. It was your baby, wasn't it?"

She watched the muscle leap in his jaw, then the movement of his Adam's apple as he swallowed. "Yes." His reply came in a hoarse whisper.

Marissa blinked at the thin film of tears and walked silently to him. This was her older brother, who had always been so strong and unemotional. Yet if he had cried loud and vocally, she wouldn't have been more affected than she was at that moment. Somehow Marissa had known Deke needed someone. She hadn't hugged her brother since her preteenage days, but she put her arms around him now.

"I'm sorry, Deke," she whispered and felt him shudder.

"It was my fault." His voice was half-muffled. "She was running from me when she fell down the stairs. Oh, God, Marissa—" he choked up and pulled away from her, turning to move to the window and regain control.

There was a lot more to the story, but Marissa didn't think it was the time to talk about it. "I brought you some clean clothes. The nurse said there's a place where you can shower and change." She paused, then added, "You'll feel better."

He half-turned and appeared ready to argue, then gave in with a nod. "Okay."

Her lashes felt very heavy when Angie tried to open them. The pain was excruciating. It felt like someone was trying to split her head open with an axe. The first second, everything looked blurred. Then she managed to focus her gaze on the man standing beside her bed. Gray-haired, he was wearing one of those white medical jackets over his business suit. He was writing something on a clipboard. Angie frowned, trying to fight through the pain to figure out where she was. The man glanced at her through the lenses of his eyeglasses.

"I see you have blue eyes, Miss Hall," he remarked with a half-smile. "I was wondering what color they were. How are you feeling this morning?" The faint smile seemed to reach his eyes. "Probably like someone who's fallen down a flight of stairs, I imagine."

Angie tried to nod, remembering what had happened, but the movement sent a shaft of pain through her head. She tried to raise her hand, but it made her aware of more aches.

"Your head hurts, doesn't it?" the doctor observed. "You banged it pretty good when you fell. That headache should go away after a few days, but we'll give you something for the pain in the meantime."

As long as she didn't try to move her head, the pain seemed bearable. Her lips felt parched and thick. Angie tried to moisten them, but it was difficult to get them to function.

"You've cracked a couple of ribs, so I wouldn't do too much laughing for awhile if I were you," the doctor joked.

Her mouth curved into a weak smile at his attempt at humor. Something didn't feel right. Then she knew it had to do with the life she had carried inside her. She looked at the doctor, her blue eyes expressive in their silent question. Her hand moved tentatively toward her stomach in a belated gesture of protection.

"My baby?" Her voice was hardly more than a croaking sound.

"I'm sorry." His smile was amazingly gentle. "You suffered a miscarriage from the fall." Tears welled in her eyes and slid slowly off her lashes. Angie tried to avert her head, but it hurt too much. "There's no reason to think you can't have more children." The doctor attempted to comfort her with that knowledge. "There's a gentleman who is probably more capable of cheering you up than I am, so I'll leave you two alone." At Angie's questioning look, he smiled, "I'll be in to see you tomorrow."

Her gaze went past him and noticed Deke standing in the foreground. He seemed a little gaunt-cheeked, but otherwise his appearance was fresh and crisp. There was a shadowed darkness to his eyes that didn't let her see inside. Angie ached for him to take her in his arms and share her tears for the baby they'd lost. But he hadn't wanted the baby. She remembered how angry he'd been when she told him.

Regardless of the pain it caused, Angie turned her face away from him. Her head felt as if it was breaking into as many pieces as her heart. There was so much pain throbbing through her that she felt like one big ache. She wanted to close her eyes and shut it all out, drift back into that black world where she hadn't known anything.

"Angie." The husky pitch of Deke's voice wrenched at her heart. It was all she could do not to look at him. "Please. I'm sorry."

Her throat was constricted so tightly that it hurt to talk, but she forced the words out. "I don't want your pity, Deke."

"It was my fault." His low voice continued, rough with guilt. "I shouldn't have tried to stop you. I should have let you go."

Oh, God, she hated him for being so damned noble and taking the blame for her fall. She didn't want him to feel tied to her out of some sense of responsibility. That was why they had argued, because he had felt honor-bound to marry her because she was carrying his child. Duty was a poor replacement for love.

"It doesn't matter," Angie rejected his penitent confession.

She felt him take her hand and lay it in the palm of his. Her sharply indrawn breath sent a stab of pain through her ribcage, a pointed reminder of the cracked ribs. As her arm stiffened to pull her hand away, Deke tightened his hold on it and stroked it with his other hand, an evocative caress that soothed and comforted.

"When you're released from the hospital, Angie, will you let me look after you?" he asked huskily. "I want to take care of you."

The timbre of his voice was too persuasive and Angie felt too vulnerable. Deke could so easily twist her into knots with his kindness if she let him. And she mustn't let herself be swayed by his well-meant intentions into giving in. She didn't dare listen to him.

"Deke, please." Her voice was pleading. "Just go away."

She started crying silently, sobs shaking her body and causing more pain to compound her anguish. Biting her lip, Angie tried to stop the stream of tears from her eyes. His hold had tightened its grip on hers and she tried to twist out of it, but he was lifting her hand and enclosing it between his.

"Angie—"

When she felt the warmth of his mouth near her fingers, she protested bitterly. "Leave me alone!"

This time Deke didn't resist her attempt to pull her hand free. She sensed his movement away from the bed, but he didn't leave the room. She could feel him watching her, and that was equally agonizing. Then the door opened, and there was the rustle of a uniform. Angie looked up as a nurse stopped beside the bed. Despite her briskly professional air as she swabbed a spot on Angie's upper arm, her keenly observant eyes had a gentle quality when they swept Angie's face.

"I have a little something here for the pain," she told Angie. The stinging prick of the hypodermic needle was minor compared to the rest of her aches. It was followed by a brief sensation of something surging into her blood, then it was over. "You rest," the nurse ordered with a slight smile.

"Yes," Angie whispered, welcoming whatever promise of relief it offered.

The nurse moved away from the bed, but before she left the room, Angie heard her murmur to Deke, "She'll sleep for awhile."

Angie closed her eyes, aware that Deke hadn't taken the hint and left the room. It wasn't too much longer when she felt soft, puffy clouds enfolding her mind and hazing her thoughts. She embraced the nothingness with open arms. Deke couldn't go where she was going, so she escaped from him—released at last from all sensation.

Her fork pushed the food around on the hospital tray. Angie tried another bite and chewed it slowly without tasting it. Finally she put her fork down, not hungry and unable to force any more food down. Her gaze wandered out the window of the hospital room to absently study the pattern of long shadows cast by a setting sun.

At the sound of the door opening, Angie sent a disinterested glance in its direction. She expected to see the nurse's aide coming to collect her tray. Her eyes widened in surprise when she recognized the tall brunette enter- 'ing her room.

"Marissa," she murmured in vague disbe- lief.

A wide smile attempted to mask the bright concern in her eyes as Marissa approached the bed, carrying a gift-wrapped box and a small case. She glanced at the tray in front of Angie.

"They're letting you eat real food," she ob- served. "That's a good sign." Marissa peered at the tray's contents. "It smells good, but you haven't eaten much."

"I'm not hungry," Angie dismissed that sub- ject to stare at her visitor. "What are you doing here?"

"I have come bearing gifts," she declared, and wheeled aside the stand to present Angie with a beribboned box. "One gift, at least. It's from Lindy and me. Open it," she urged.

Angie untied the bright yellow ribbon and worked off the lid of the cardboard box. The contents were hidden in layers of tissue paper. When she finally pushed them all aside, she uncovered an elegant bedjacket of lilac satin.

"I guess I don't have to tell you that Lindy picked it out," Marissa said.

"It's beautiful." Angie fingered the slick material of the ruffled collar.

"I'll help you put it on," Marissa volun- teered, taking it out of the box. "I thought you'd probably be tired of these drab hospital gowns, and like something a little more feminine to wear." She helped Angie slip an arm in the sleeve and hesitated at the sight of a large black and blue bruise. "That's a beauty, isn't it? It clashes a little with this lavender jacket," she teased. "There," she buttoned the front and stepped back to admire the result. "You look great."

"Thank you," Angie murmured, still a little dazed that Marissa was actually there.

And Marissa was rushing right along, not giving her a chance to ask anything. "The nurse said they were going to have you up and walking tomorrow," she smiled, then appeared to remember the small travel case she'd set on the foot of the bed. "I packed a few things that I thought you might need— makeup, *et cetera*. If I've forgotten anything, just let me know."

"Marissa," A worried frown touched her forehead. "Does Deke know you're here?" Angie had to find out.

"Yes. Lindy and I flew in from Dallas last night as soon as I heard about your accident," she replied. *Dallas, that's where they were*, Angie thought. "Deke's back at the ranch— sleeping, hopefully," Marissa explained as if Angie had been wondering where he was instead of being relieved that he wasn't there. "That brother of mine was absolutely glued to that chair all the while you were unconscious. Didn't eat and wouldn't sleep."

Angie looked down at the hospital sheet. "He blames himself for what happened," she said flatly.

"Yes, I know," Marissa replied. "I poured a couple shots of whiskey down him. In his condition, that was all it took. Before he passed out, he mentioned he'd been arguing with you." There was a slight pause. "Do you blame him, Angie?"

"No. It simply happened. It wasn't anyone's fault." She made it very clear to his sister that she didn't want Deke to feel responsible. The accident didn't put him under any obligation to her. "How's Lindy?" Angie changed the subject to a topic less painful than a discussion of Deke.

"She's fine—glad to be home. I tried to let you know what was happening," Marissa began.

"I know." Angie didn't want to talk about that either.

"If all goes well, you should be released from the hospital the day after tomorrow." This time Marissa changed the subject. "Why don't you come to the ranch and recuperate there? It will be a perfect opportunity for you to get acquainted with Lindy."

Angie tensed, flashing her friend a sharp glance. "Does Deke know about this? Was it his idea?"

"I suggested it to him and he agreed." Marissa eyed her curiously.

On the surface, it appeared to be a thoughtful invitation, but Angie knew that Deke was motivated by a desire to make up to her for the accident. He wanted to alleviate his guilt. But it would be disastrous for her to be around him. She loved him so, and if he was kind to her, she might be tempted into settling for something less than the relationship she wanted.

"Deke isn't sending Lindy away again?" Angie questioned.

"No," Marissa replied, and left it to Angie to read between the lines that she had Deke's permission to be with her daughter. "Jessie— our housekeeper—is getting the bedroom next to Lindy's all ready for you."

"No. I won't be going to the ranch after I'm released," Angie stated in a firm denial of the invitation. "And you can give Deke a message for me. Tell him I'm not going to chase any more carrots." Because she knew he had dangled Lindy in front of her again.

"But—" Marissa was frowning. "Where will you go? Back to the summer house?"

"No." She didn't want to go there either— not where she had lived with Deke . . . practically as man and wife. There were too many painful memories attached to that house. "I'll stay in a motel for a few days until I decide what I'm going to do. Marissa, would you do me a favor?" There was a kind of desperation in the look she gave the brunette.

"Name it," she agreed without hesitation.

"I would prefer not to . . . go back to the summer house," Angie explained hesitantly. "Would you pack my clothes for me and put the rest of my things in storage for the time being?"

"If that's what you want." Marissa wore a

slightly puzzled frown. "But what about you and Deke?"

"It's over between us," Angie said. "It's finished—for the last and final time.

But when Deke came through that hospital room door the next morning, Angie knew it wasn't finished. You couldn't stop loving a person at will. Her heart gave a painful leap at the sight of him, so lean and ruggedly handsome in a western-cut suit. He was carrying a bouquet of roses—red roses for love. Angie reminded herself in time that it was just a gesture. The color had no meaning to him, except it was what the florist had on hand.

He stopped by her bed and removed his hat to hold it at his side. His proud features seemed totally devoid of expression and there was a haunting blankness to his gray eyes. Her head throbbed at the thought that she would never touch him again, never feel his arms around her, never taste the hard warmth of his mouth. Angie glimpsed the lonely agony that was ahead of her.

"I brought you some flowers," Deke said quietly.

"They're very lovely." It was a stilted answer. Angie knew she didn't dare reach for them. She was shaking so badly inside that it was certain to show. "You can put them on the bedside table."

He hesitated, then placed them on the stand

next to her bed. "How are you feeling today?" His gaze made a searching study of her face, noting the pallor and the strained blankness.

"I'm much better, thank you," she replied, not looking at him.

"Marissa tells me that you turned down the invitation to recuperate at the ranch." His tone asked for confirmation.

"That's right." Her glance ricocheted off his face and returned to her bed covers.

"It wasn't a carrot, Angie." There was a taut edge to his voice. "I meant it when I said I wanted to take care of you."

"I can take care of myself," she retorted. "I don't want you to look after me."

There was an oppressive tension in the air. Angie had trouble breathing the heavy atmosphere; her lungs hurt with the effort. Her eyes burned from the concentrated interest she was focusing on the fold in the sheet. Finally, Deke turned away from the bed and walked to the window. Her gaze followed him and studied his uplifted profile, starkly masculine and strong. He laid an arm high on the window frame, bracing himself with it. His hat remained tightly clenched at his thigh.

"I won't keep you from seeing Lindy." His voice seemed to come from far away. "She can visit you whenever you like—weekends, holidays." He drank in a deep breath and studied the blue sky outside the window. "I know this doesn't make up for what I've done to you, but I never meant it to turn out this way. I'm sorry, Angie."

"We are both sorry about a lot of things, Deke." Her throat ached from the effort to speak.

"I won't trouble you again." He turned from the window and looked at the hat he gripped with both hands. Then he was pushing it on his head. "Goodbye, Angie."

She had one glimpse of his hard, chiseled features before Deke walked out the door. "Goodbye," she choked on a half-sob. It sounded so final now. She couldn't stop wishing that it could have ended some other way. She turned her face into the pillow and cried for what they could have had—if he had loved her.

Deke didn't come again to visit her in the hospital. Angie forced herself not to ask Marissa about him when she came to see her. She kept telling herself to keep the break clean. It would mend quicker that way. But there was excruciating pain that went with the healing process.

Chapter Thirteen

Two days later, Angie was dismissed from the hospital. The bandage had been removed from the gash on her forehead and her bruises were all turning a yellowish-green. There continued to be a dull throb in her head, but otherwise, she was as physically healthy as the hospital could make her.

Marissa waited for her while Angie signed all the necessary papers for her discharge. When she had finished, Marissa insisted on carrying her travel case out to the car. The roses Deke had given her, Angie left behind. She didn't want any flowers that symbolized a love that had never been hers.

Too preoccupied with her own thoughts, Angie didn't notice Marissa's silence during the drive to the motel where she'd be staying. If anything, she regarded it as a relief not to have to make idle conversation. Marissa stopped the car in front of the motel office, but she didn't turn off the engine.

"Angie." She turned her head. "Have I ever asked you to do anything for me?"

The question puzzled her, so did the worried concern she saw in Marissa's eyes. "No."

"I wouldn't ask you now if I thought there was anyone else who could help," she explained. "But I'm at my wit's end."

"What is it?" Angie could see she was sincerely upset. "Is it Lindy?"

"No—it's Deke." She saw Angie stiffen at his name and hurried. "I know you said it was finished between you two, but—Angie, he hasn't been to the ranch since he talked to you at the hospital. He's at the summer house." Angie looked away, nearly overwhelmed by the urge to run. "He just sits there, Angie. He won't talk. Nothing." Marissa paused as if seeking a way to explain. "I've even taken Lindy there to see him, thinking that he would snap out of it, but he just walks into another room and shuts the door. I've tried everything and I can't seem to reach him."

"I can't help you," Angie said flatly.

"You've got to," Marissa insisted. "Deke is obviously blaming himself for what happened. If you would talk to him, make him understand that you have forgiven him—or something. Angie, that's all I'm asking," she pleaded. "I'm frightened. I've never seen him like this before. Please, he might listen to you."

How could she refuse? It was impossible. Angie sighed heavily in defeat. "All right. I'll talk to him, but you come with me."

"I will." She reached out to squeeze Angie's hand in gratitude. "Thank you."

A half dozen times on the way to the Key, Angie changed her mind. Her palms were sweating when Marissa turned the car into the driveway of the summer house and her head was starting to pound again. At first she didn't notice the small group of neighbors clustered in the adjoining yard, all her attention focused on the house where she'd lived with Deke. When she stepped out of the car to join Marissa, the elderly neighbor, Mrs. Osborne, split from the others to come over.

"I am so glad you are here, Marissa," she declared. "There has been the most awful racket going on inside the house. We weren't sure what we should do."

Marissa cast an anxious glance at Angie, then assured the neighbor. "We'll check it out, Mrs. Osborne."

"Maybe my husband should go inside with you," the woman suggested.

"I'm sure we'll be all right," Marissa murmured.

Concern for Deke overwhelmed any personal fears for herself as Angie walked swiftly to the door. The house was quiet when she entered just a step ahead of Marissa. She climbed the stairs to the living quarters, listening intently for any sound.

When she crossed the threshold at the top of the stairs, there was a fleeting memory of that last angry scene before she'd fallen. It vanished the instant she looked into the living room. She was stopped short by the shambles the room was in. Furniture was turned over, chairs and tables were broken, and the drapes were half-ripped from their rods.

"What happened?" Marissa breathed in stunned shock.

"I don't know." Angie finally moved, her legs shaking.

The dining room was in a similar state of destruction. The kitchen seemed relatively untouched, although appliances were scattered on the floor as if someone had swept them off the counter.

"I think we'd better call the police," Marissa murmured, shaken by the vandal-like destruction in the house. She moved uncertainly toward the phone on the wall, stepping over an electric toaster on the floor.

"But where is Deke?" Angie frowned, worried now about him. "If he was here when whoever did this—" She didn't finish the sentence afraid to put it into words as she and Marissa exchanged a frightened look. "Let's check the bedrooms first."

"Okay," Marissa agreed, but with some misgivings.

They had barely left the kitchen when a loud thump came from another part of the house. Alarm shot through Angie's nerves at the sound. It came from the bedroom area. Her stride faltered for an instant, caution briefly surfacing to slow her.

"What was that?" Marissa whispered.

"I don't know." But her mind could only think about Deke.

Angie broke into a running walk as she hurried down the hallway with Marissa directly behind her. The doors to the bedrooms stood open, but none of them appeared to have suffered the destruction of the front rooms. Angie did no more than glance in them as she went by to confirm that Deke wasn't there. The closed door of the master bedroom acted as a beacon, signaling to her. Angie didn't slow down until she reached it. For a short second, she paused to listen, her hand poised on the knob, but no sound came from inside the room.

Behind her, Marissa crowded close, offering the reassurance of her presence. Turning the knob, she pushed the door open an inch at a time, her heart pounding like a trip-hammer in her chest. Her first views of the room mirrored the destruction that had befallen the front rooms. Bedding was torn off the bed, the framework was broken, sending the mattress and springs askew. Drawers were pulled out of the dresser—a couple of them were smashed.

When she saw Deke kneeling in the middle of the chaos, the breath she'd been holding was released in a sighing sob of relief. Her gaze ran over his hunched figure, but his bowed head kept her from seeing his face. Something was clutched in his hands, its blue color vaguely familiar to Angie. The identity of it was completely unimportant at the moment. While there were no outward indications that he was injured, the impression was of a man in intense pain.

It was Marissa who finally broke Angie's semi-paralysis by shouldering past her to enter the room. "My God, Deke, are you all right?" Her alarmed question was followed instantly by another as his sister sent a disbelieving look around the room. "What happened here?"

Her voice was slow to create a reaction from her brother, but when it did, Deke came to his feet like a raging bull. His sudden fury took them both by surprise, shocking them into stillness.

"Get out of here!" Deke roared, a wounded, snarling animal with his teeth bared and his features contorted with the rage of agony.

The instant his blazing gray eyes saw Angie standing near the door, his expression changed to that of a demented man, haunted by hallucinations. He stared, clinging to the mirage before him. Raw emotion burned in his eyes while the wetness of tears brought a sheen to his high cheekbones. Angie was gripped by the sight of him, her heart squeezed until it matched the pain she saw. She took a step toward him, and the movement seemed to break the spell of illusion that had paralyzed him. She was real, not a spectre come to haunt him.

"Deke, are you all right?" Angie murmured anxiously.

It seemed to take great effort and will for him to tear his gaze from her. Its downward focus finally centered on the article clenched in his hand. His fist tightened on it.

"I suppose this is what you came for." When he spoke, his voice seemed to come from some deep pit. "It was overlooked in the packing." With a suddenly violent emotion, Deke hurled it at Angie. "Take it and go."

Through sheer reflex, she caught it while her stunned gaze watched him stride to the glass doors that opened onto the private balcony. She looked down at the cloth in her hands and recognized the blue silk of her favorite blouse. It had been in the laundry— laundry that was now scattered over the floor, the clothes hamper overturned and partially smashed. Marissa must have missed it when she packed her things. Angie's confusion mounted. Why had Deke been clutching it? What did it mean? Her questioning gaze ran back to his broad-shouldered figure, his back turned to her as he faced the balcony. She glanced at Marissa whose concern for her brother was more deeply etched in her face. But his sister offered no answers to her questions.

"Deke—" Angie tried again to appeal to him for an explanation.

"Get out of here!" He cast a snarling look over his shoulder. "Both of you!"

Angie recoiled from the savagery in his loud voice and twisted features. If he had physically slapped her, Deke couldn't have made it plainer that she wasn't wanted here. Trembling, she looked at the blouse in her hands. She blessed the dryness of her eyes, incapable of shedding any more tears. She made a move to leave, but the touch of Marissa's hand on her arm stayed her.

"Please talk to him, Angie," Marissa appealed to her again and glanced at her brother, then bowed her head. "I'll wait for you in the other room," she murmured, then lifted her teary gaze. "He'll listen to you. I know he will. Please."

After Marissa had quietly exited the room and closed the door to give them privacy, Angie looked at the solid wall of Deke's back and wasn't so sure. There was more than the width of the room separating them, but it was the easiest to cross, regardless of the obstacle course of broken furniture and scattered laundry.

Deke seemed oblivious to her presence—a statue carved out of teakwood, set facing the glass doors. The rough masculine features of his profile were etched in sharp relief, tanned skin stretched across hard sinew and bone.

"Deke, what is it?" Angie didn't understand.

"Will you go away?" His voice was hard and

taut as he refused to look at her. "Just go away." She could see the muscles working in his jaw, controlling whatever emotion that was churning inside.

"Will you please tell me what it is?" Angie repeated her question, trying desperately to reach him—to persuade him to release the thing he was holding inside.

When Deke turned his head to look at her, she was close enough to see that his eyes looked bloodshot and raw. It was a frightening sight of a man half-crazed with pain. She wanted to cry for him as if her tears could soothe his reddened eyes.

"Why are you here? Why did you come?" His questions were forced through his tightly clenched jaw.

His fiercely pained gaze scanned her face, looking for something. Was it blame as his sister had suggested? But she didn't hold him responsible for the miscarriage. Surely he could see that.

"Marissa asked me to come," she admitted frankly. "She thought it might help if I talked to you."

His face went cold and he turned away. "She wasted your time. We have nothing left to talk about." His voice was brutally harsh, leaving her in no doubt that he was through with her. "You wanted permission to see Lindy—you've got it. You wanted independence—you're free. You didn't want to remain here—so leave. What is left to discuss?"

"You," Angie replied with quiet intensity. "And what you're doing to yourself!"

"Surely that's my business!" Deke snapped.

"Marissa said you haven't been to the ranch for days," she accused.

"It'll survive without me." He continued to stare out the window, tight-lipped and coldly contained.

"For how long?" Angie challenged him softly.

"What do you care?" Deke blazed suddenly, showing how tenuous his control was, and launched himself away from the window—and Angie. His long strides carried him to the center of the room and no farther. A rigid tension held him motionless.

"What about the people who depend on you?" she reasoned. "Marissa, Lindy and the men on the ranch who work for you."

She approached him slowly with caution. The impression was strong that he was a wounded animal, capable of turning on her, not caring that she only wanted to help.

"They can look after themselves," Deke replied grimly.

"Lindy, too?" she murmured.

"Lindy's got you." The thickness of thinning patience was heavy in his voice. "Will you get out of here?!"

He wasn't listening to her. He was shutting her out. What had she expected? She had been wrong to listen to Marissa. Angie looked around the room, seeing again the destruction so similar to the rest of the house.

"What happened here, Deke?" She voiced her confusion. "Who did this?"

"Who the hell do you think?" He turned on her, his rage barely controlled. "I did!" Deke paused, straining for words and control. He turned away and expelled a weary, frustrated breath. "Please go."

She had suspected he'd done it, but she hadn't wanted to admit it until she'd heard him say it. But she still didn't understand.

"Why, Deke?" Her head moved from side to side as she groped helplessly for a reason. "Why?"

"Why the hell do you think?" The response was dragged from him. "Because I couldn't stand to look at it any more and remember." His gaze swung to her, some kind of hunger in their scanning look. "I can't even stand to be around my own daughter," he declared hoarsely. "Every time I look at her, I see you. And it just tears me apart all over again."

She searched his face for an incredulous second, certain that she was misunderstanding. "What are you saying?" Angie breathed.

"I let you go out of my life once, Angie, and survived," Deke murmured thickly. "But I don't think I can make it a second time." There was a dejected shake of his head. "I tried. I really thought I could do it."

"Marissa thought . . . I thought you were blaming yourself because I lost the baby," Angie whispered, but he seemed to be saying that wasn't the cause for his erratic behavior at all.

"That *was* my fault." Deke turned from her, hanging his head. Pain was creased into the drawn, white features of his profile. Angie was shaken by the sensation she was looking at a broken man.

"I fell, Deke. It was an *accident*," she insisted.

"You fell because you were running from me," he corrected and lifted his hands to look at them, palms upward, fingers spread. There was strength in their calloused dimensions. "I might as well have pushed you down those stairs with these two hands."

"That isn't true," Angie protested, but nothing she said seemed to mean anything to him.

"It is." His eyes were tightly closed as he forced the assertion through gritted teeth. "I drove you away from me and killed our baby at the same time."

"Deke, stop it." She was trembling, racked by the pain and guilt that was twisting inside him. "Stop torturing yourself with this."

When her hand touched his arm in an attempt to turn him around so she could see his face, Deke reacted with the same violence she'd seen in him earlier. He swung around, severing the contact with a wild shrug of his arm.

"Don't do that!" Deke thundered in a raw frenzy. Angie recoiled from him, and his rage dissipated in a shudder. "For God's sake, don't touch me. Have some pity."

He was so vulnerable, so easily hurt that

she wanted to cry for him. "I do," Angie murmured with an ache in her voice for him.

"Go away," he groaned. "Can't you see it's worse with you here?"

"No, I'm not leaving—not yet," Angie insisted, but she couldn't leave him in this state. "Not until you realize that you weren't responsible for my accident. You're feeling guilty because you didn't want the baby, not because we lost it."

"Not want the baby?!" There was an incredulous ring in his hoarse voice. "How could I *not* want it? It was yours and mine!"

"But—" Confusion darkened her eyes as Angie raked a hand through her hair. "—you were angry when I told you I was pregnant."

"Yes, I was angry," Deke admitted huskily, desperation clawing through his voice and expression. "It was all happening again. I'd gotten you pregnant with a baby you didn't want."

"But I *wanted* it." She breathed out the words, stunned by his explanation.

"Don't say that." He turned his head from her. "Don't make it worse than it is."

"Deke, I wanted the baby," Angie insisted, refusing to pretend otherwise. "The same as I wanted Lindy when I was pregnant with her. But I thought you didn't."

"In God's name, why would you think such a thing?" His gray eyes were nearly black with hurt from her accusation.

This time, she was the one who looked away. "Deke, please don't try to convince me

242

that you would have asked me to marry you if I hadn't told you I was pregnant. I'll never believe it." She felt the sting of tears in her eyes.

"I wouldn't have asked you that night," he admitted. "Maybe it would have been months before I realized that I wouldn't be satisfied with anything less. I just knew I had to keep you here—any way I could."

Her gaze ran back to him, wary of false hope. Yet, there seemed to be something more than just desire in his hungry look. Angie could almost see the light glimmering at the end of her long, lonely tunnel.

"Why?" she whispered.

"Because I can't make it without you." He looked extremely tired, defeated. "I don't even have the strength to try this time."

He had said almost the same thing earlier, only she hadn't been ready to believe him. Now, she was slowly accepting that he meant it. He wasn't just saying it to assuage any guilt for the accident.

"The night of the accident, I was running away from you because I didn't want you to marry me out of a sense of responsibility," Angie told him.

"I was responsible for you being pregnant," Deke reminded her tersely.

"So was I," she asserted. "I'm not a naive teenager anymore, so I can't pretend an ignorance of the precautions to avoid becoming pregnant. I was equally responsible for my condition."

"What does it matter now?" he argued wearily. "I still caused you to lose the child. You've admitted you were running from me."

"Yes. I debated whether I should even tell you I was pregnant," Angie admitted. "I considered seriously taking advantage of the fact you were gone and leaving before you found out. In the end, I realized I had to tell you. I hoped . . . you might be happy about it, because it could have meant we had a chance together. Instead, you were angry."

"Not about the baby." Deke was frowning, his gaze narrowed in its haunted study of her. "It was your face when you told me—the way you looked at me—" He stopped, not finishing the sentence.

"I don't understand," she murmured in bewilderment.

"Remember the time when you asked me how much more I expected you to give—that I'd taken your pride and self-respect by installing you in this house as my mistress?" His mouth thinned into a line of self-disgust.

"I remember," Angie nodded faintly.

"I replied that I wanted you to give yourself," Deke reminded her. "I wanted revenge for the hell I went through when you left me the last time. I was determined that you were going to suffer the same agony that I did."

She was stunned by his confession that his cruelty had been deliberate, then skillfully disguised it. "You never had any intention of letting me see Lindy. It was all a lie when you claimed we needed to get to know each other before you would give your consent to that."

"It was all a lie." His stark, powerful features were riddled with contempt for his perfidy.

Never once had Angie suspected the extent of his deceit and premeditation. She had always given him the benefit of a doubt, convinced he was only testing the sincerity of her motives. She was staggered by how wrong she'd been.

"How could you?" Angie whispered brokenly. "You let me think—"

"I know." His broad chest heaved with a deep breath. The gauntness around his face and eyes became more pronounced. "If I destroyed you, I guess I thought it would crush the need I had for you. Only it didn't work."

"It's all been a lie." Her gaze swung away from him and stopped on the mattress, tilted on its broken frame. "All those nights we slept together in this bed, you were just—"

"—trying to get you out of my system," Deke finished the sentence before she could reach a different conclusion. "I didn't think there was anything left of what I'd felt for you . . . until you showed up here again. When I realized you could still arouse my lust, I hated myself for not having the strength to resist you. Everytime I was near you, I wanted you—day or night."

"So you brought me here—where I could be at your disposal." Angie felt cheap and used, more so than she had before, because there weren't any more doubts about his attitude toward her.

"I tried to pretend that my needs were only sexual—except that—it was always more than sex with us," he stated. "I found myself wanting to spend all my time here—with you. I wanted your company, not just in bed, but at the dinner table, behind the counter in the mornings fixing my breakfast, by my side walking along the beach—all the time, in any situation. I resented that, too."

She listened to him, trying to believe that he meant it, because that's the way it had been for her, too. If he was lying now, she wanted to die.

"You have every reason to hate me," he declared in a resigned voice.

"It hurts." Her throat ached with the words.

"When you fell down those steps, I saw what I'd done to you—to us. I knew you couldn't forgive me, not after the way I treated you." Pain flashed through his expression. "I killed the chance you could ever care for me, the same way I killed our baby."

"It wasn't your fault I lost the baby," Angie insisted again.

But Deke wasn't listening. "I tried to make it up to you. That's why I gave you permission to see Lindy any time you wanted. It was wrong to keep holding onto you when you wanted your freedom. I tried to give you everything you wanted."

"Not everything." She shook her head to

indicate his failure. "I wanted your love, Deke. It would have made up for everything."

Doubt clouded his eyes. "You've always had my love. I never stopped loving you—not even during all those years we were apart."

"I didn't think you loved me when we were married," Angie remembered. "You didn't act like you did."

"How could I?" he frowned. "You wouldn't share that single bed with me at your uncle's house. I couldn't find an apartment that pleased you. You gave me no indication that you wanted my kisses. What was I supposed to do?" he demanded. "Assert my conjugal rights? Raping my pregnant wife?"

"I didn't think you loved me then. And when you announced we were getting married because I was pregnant again, I ran away to escape another forced marriage without love," she explained. "I was afraid you'd be able to convince me it would work out."

Deke took an involuntary step toward her. "Could I have convinced you, Angie?" He searched her face.

Her laugh was a breathless sound, dry and without humor. "Too easily," she admitted. "Oh, don't you see?" Her chin quivered with emotion. "I had finally stopped kidding myself that I was only staying here because of Lindy. It might have started out, partially, that way, but I stayed because I was in love with you."

For a split second, Deke didn't move. Then he gathered her roughly into his arms and buried his face against the side of her neck.

She clung to him, pressing herself to his length. Warm tears slipped from her lashes to run down her cheeks, but they were tears of joy, multiplying with love returned in equal measure.

"Don't leave me, Angie," Deke muttered thickly against her skin. "I'll go crazy without you."

"I'll never leave you," she promised and tried to absorb the shudders that trembled through him. "Not ever again."

With a stifled moan, his mouth covered her lips, kissing her deeply and hungrily. A golden fire of emotion flamed them together. His hands moved restlessly over her flesh, shaping her curves to his male body and sending stimulating signals through her bones. Angie quivered with the sweet intensity of belonging to him, shaken by the rough insistence of his exploring hands.

This new certainty of each other brought its own magic to their embrace. It twined around them, binding them with love and surrendering them to its demands.

An unexpected pain pierced through Angie, causing her to gasp sharply. Deke instantly relaxed the tight band of his encircling arms to ease the pressure on her injured ribs. His beard-growth scratched her cheek as he rubbed his jaw against it, but Angie didn't draw his attention to that minor discomfort, strangely enjoying the rasping caress.

"I'm sorry. I didn't mean to hurt you," he declared roughly and shuddered again.

"Everything I do seems to end up hurting you."

"Your love doesn't hurt. It turns all the pain into a little ache." She drew her head back and curved her hand against his cheek. "I almost didn't come today. If Marissa hadn't convinced me, I'm not sure what would have happened."

"I can tell you one thing." The silver brilliance of his eyes burned over her up-turned face. "This house wouldn't be here. I would have torn it down with my own two hands."

"Is that what you were trying to do in here?" A hint of a smile touched her mouth, remembering the destruction throughout the house.

"Initially, I was trying to exorcise your ghost from this place," Deke admitted. "But when I reached the bedroom, I knew it wouldn't work. The whole building had to be demolished. Even then, it wouldn't get you out of my heart, or my head."

"Mine, either."

His hand trembled as he traced a tentative finger over her cheek where a tear had left a wet streak. "I would make love to you, Angie," he said thickly. "But I know it's too soon after you've lost the baby."

"Just hold me. It's enough for now," she murmured.

"No, it isn't enough just to hold you," Deke refused to accept that. "It won't be enough until you're wearing my ring on your finger. Will you marry me, Angie?"

"Yes." The simplicity of her answer was poignantly sufficient.

Deke started to kiss her, but a light knock on the bedroom door interrupted him. It surprised Angie, too. She had forgotten they weren't alone in the house. She was too used to them being the sole occupants.

"It's Marissa, I think," she murmured in response to his frowning glance at the door. "She was going to wait outside for me. I imagine she's anxious because I've been in here so long."

"Shall I tell her to go away?" There was a trace of his former mocking charm in the glitter of his eyes.

The second knock was a bit more assertive than the first. "She's been very worried about you," Angie reminded him.

Deke sighed, and reluctantly called, "Come in."

The door was hesitantly opened and Marissa glanced in. Her expression was apprehensive about what she might see, and it slowly cleared with relief when she saw Angie lovingly enfolded in her brother's arms.

"Is everything all right?" she asked to be sure.

"It's better than all right," Deke stated and studied Angie with an open possessiveness. "Angie has agreed to marry me."

"I hoped—" Marissa could barely contain her delight at the news. "I'm so glad it turned out this way. I was so sure you both loved each other."

"We do." Angie had just as much difficulty as Deke in looking at anyone else.

"What about Lindy? What will you tell her?" Marissa wondered.

"First, we'll let her get used to the idea that she'll soon be having a mother as well as a father," Deke said, watching Angie to be certain she agreed with his plan. "Then, we'll sit down with her and explain the whole story to her. Angie is her mother. And it's important for Lindy to know that, even though it will be hard for her to understand in the beginning."

"We can wait until she's older, if you think it would be easier for her," Angie said.

"No." There was a firm shake of his head. "Our daughter has very keen hearing. She's liable to eavesdrop on a private conversation. We'll be honest with her—the way we should have been with each other.

"You're right," she agreed.

"Marissa," Deke spoke to his sister without looking at her. "I know I owe you a great deal for persuading Angie to come here today, and for introducing me to her in the first place, but why don't you get lost for a couple of hours. Go back to the ranch or something."

"I will," Marissa smiled, yet didn't make any immediate move to leave. "Except you should know that the police are outside."

Both of them looked at her. "The police?" Deke repeated. "What do they want?"

"Mrs. Osborne got worried when Angie and I didn't come out right away. After all the racket she and the neighbors heard before we arrived, she decided to call the police in case something had happened to us," his sister explained.

Deke released a heavy sigh. "I suppose I'll have to assure them that everything is all right."

"Shall I come with you?" Angie volunteered.

"No." He pressed a hard kiss on her lips. "Just be here waiting for me when I come back."

"Always," she promised.

Silhouette Special Edition

MORE ROMANCE FOR
A SPECIAL WAY TO RELAX

Have you missed a title by your favourite author? Is your collection incomplete? This is your opportunity to purchase the Silhouette Special Edition novels you may have missed.

Simply check (✓) the novels you require on the listing below and mail with your cheque to

Silhouette Book Club of Canada
P.O. Box 910, 517 Lorne Ave.
Stratford, Ont. N5A 6W2

TITLE NO.	TITLE	AUTHOR
5 ☐	Paradise Postponed	Jane Converse
6 ☐	Search For A New Dawn	Billie Douglass
7 ☐	Silver Mist	Sondra Stanford
8 ☐	Keys To Daniels House	Carole Halston
9 ☐	All Our Tomorrows	Mary Lynn Baxter
10 ☐	Texas Rose	Kathryn Thiels
11 ☐	Love Is Surrender	Carolyn Thornton
12 ☐	Never Give Your Heart	Tracy Sinclair
13 ☐	Bitter Victory	Patti Beckman
14 ☐	Eye Of The Hurricane	Sarah Keene
15 ☐	Dangerous Magic	Stephanie James
16 ☐	Mayan Moon	Eleni Carr
17 ☐	So Many Tomorrows	Nancy John
18 ☐	A Womans Place	Lucy Hamilton
19 ☐	Decembers Wine	Linda Shaw
20 ☐	Northern Lights	Jacqueline Musgrave
21 ☐	Rough Diamond	Brooke Hastings
22 ☐	All That Glitters	Linda Howard
23 ☐	Love's Golden Shadow	Maggi Charles
24 ☐	Gamble Of Desire	Diana Dixon
25 ☐	Tears And Red Roses	Laura Hardy
26 ☐	A Flight Of Swallows	Joanna Scott
27 ☐	A Man With Doubts	Linda Wisdom
28 ☐	The Flaming Tree	Margaret Ripy
29 ☐	Yearning Of Angels	Fran Bergen
30 ☐	Bride In Barbados	Jeanne Stephens
31 ☐	Tears of Yesterday	Mary Lynn Baxter
32 ☐	A Time To Love	Billie Douglass
33 ☐	Heathers Song	Diana Palmer
34 ☐	Mixed Blessings	Tracy Sinclair
35 ☐	Stormy Challenge	Stephanie James

SEE REVERSE SIDE